Building the Perfect Story Brand

Make your Message More Impactful and Inspire Customers

Cole Sheehan

© **Copyright 2021 - All rights reserved.**

The content contained within this book may not be reproduced, duplicated or transmitted without direct written permission from the author or the publisher.

Under no circumstances will any blame or legal responsibility be held against the publisher, or author, for any damages, reparation, or monetary loss due to the information contained within this book, either directly or indirectly.

Legal Notice:

This book is copyright protected. It is only for personal use. You cannot amend, distribute, sell, use, quote or paraphrase any part, or the content within this book, without the consent of the author or publisher.

Disclaimer Notice:

Please note the information contained within this document is for educational and entertainment purposes only. All effort has been executed to present accurate, up to date, reliable, complete information. No warranties of any kind are declared or implied. Readers acknowledge that the author is not engaged in the rendering of legal, financial, medical or professional advice. The content within this book has been derived from various sources. Please consult a licensed professional before attempting any techniques outlined in this book.

By reading this document, the reader agrees that under no circumstances is the author responsible for any losses, direct or indirect, that are incurred as a result of the use of the information contained within this document, including, but not limited to, errors, omissions, or inaccuracies.

Table of Contents

INTRODUCTION 1

CHAPTER 1: STORYTELLING AND BUSINESS 5

IMPORTANCE OF STORYTELLING IN BUSINESS 6
- *Developing Your Business* 6
- *Gives You the Edge* 6
- *Creating a Solid Marketing Strategy* 7
- *Create an Efficient Workforce* 7

WHY SOME STORIES ARE REMEMBERED 9
HOW TO TELL THE STORY OF YOUR PRODUCT 10
- *Step 1: Identify the Protagonist* 10
- *Step 2: Show the Problem* 11
- *Step 3: Identify the Guide Who Can Lead Them to the Solution* 11
- *Step 4: Introduce a Solution* 12
- *Step 5: Show How the Solution Really Solves All Problems* 12

WHY STORYTELLING IS SUCH A POWERFUL COMMUNICATION STRATEGY 13

CHAPTER 2: BRAND STORYTELLING 17

WHAT IS BRAND STORYTELLING? 17
BRAND STORYTELLING FRAMEWORK 18
- *Who are You?* 19
- *What Are Your Products?* 19
- *Who Are Your Target Customers?* 19
- *What Are Your Ultimate Objectives?* 20
- *What is the Process?* 20

HOW CAN YOU MAKE YOUR BRAND STORY RESONATE WITH YOUR CUSTOMERS? 22
EXAMPLES OF SUCCESSFUL BRAND STORYTELLING 24
WHY BRAND STORYTELLING IS THE FUTURE OF MARKETING 25

CHAPTER 3: SELECTING YOUR NICHE THROUGH STORYTELLING 29

HOW TO DETERMINE YOUR NICHE MARKET 30
- *Determine What You are Good at* 31
- *Research Your Industry and Customer Base* 31
- *Test and Adjust Accordingly* 32

SUCCESSFUL EXAMPLES OF NICHE MARKETING 32

USING STORYTELLING TO DEFINE YOUR PROFITABLE NICHE 33
   Develop Your Social Media Voice 35
   Get Direct Feedback 35
   Create A Value Proposition 36
HOW STORYTELLING HELPS BRAND POSITIONING 37

CHAPTER 4: STORYTELLING AND MARKETING STRATEGIES 39

WHAT IS A SALES FUNNEL? 40
   Stage 1: Creating Awareness 41
   Stage 2: Invoking Interest 41
   Stage 3: Making a Decision 41
   Stage 4: The Purchase 42
HOW DOES STORYTELLING IMPROVE A SALES FUNNEL? 42
   Start with the Small Talk 43
   Dig Up Some Dirt 44
   Get Your Customer Talking 44
TELLING A STORY THROUGH COPYWRITING 45
WHAT IS NEUROMARKETING? 47
STORYTELLING IN NEUROMARKETING 48
WHY STORYTELLING IS THE BEST MARKETING STRATEGY 50

CHAPTER 5: STORYTELLING HELPS A YOUNG BUSINESS 53

LEARN HOW TO TELL YOUR STORY 53
   Connecting the Before and After Scenarios 54
   Problem-Agitate-Solve 54
   Features-Advantages-Benefits 54
   Incident-Action-Benefit 55
USING STORYTELLING IN YOUR INVESTOR PITCH 55
   Don't Bore Your Audience With Data 56
   Have An Element of Drama 56
   Emphasize on Your Points 57
   Be Spontaneous 58
MARKETING TRICKS FOR YOUR STARTUP 58
   Organize A Pre-Launch Giveaway 59
   Create Shareable Content 59
   Write a Good Marketing Copy 60
   Make Use of Visual Storytelling 60
   Hosting or Joining A Podcast 61
   Create a Rewarding Recommendation System 61
   Set up an Email Marketing Campaign 62

CHAPTER 6: A GOOD WEBSITE TELLS A GOOD STORY 65

WHY A WEBSITE IS ESSENTIAL FOR BUSINESS GROWTH 66
   Constant Online Presence and Support 66

  Availability of Information *67*
  Reduce Costs *67*
  Storytelling Redefined *67*
 D\
EVELOPING A G\
OOD W\
EBSITE 68
  Tips on Content... *69*
  Technical Development Tips *69*
  Tips on Layout *70*
  Tips on Generating Leads *70*
  Tips on Increasing Visibility *71*
 M\
AKING M\
ONEY FROM A\
FFILIATE M\
ARKETING... 72
  Benefits of Affiliate Marketing to Business Owners *73*
  Benefits of Affiliate Marketing to Bloggers *73*
  Benefits of Affiliate Marketing to Customers *74*

CONCLUSION **77**

REFERENCES... **81**

Introduction

Have you ever wondered why there is such a craze for heritage hotels all over the world? No matter what the place, heritage hotels are always in vogue. What do these places offer that is so unique? Most heritage hotels used to be castles or palaces where kings or lords lived. These old structures are renovated, restored, and converted into heritage hotels that people are obsessed with because they don't only offer a place to stay, but an experience. When you walk down the halls of a heritage hotel, you are transferred back in time. You imagine yourself to be the 'lord' or 'lady' of the castle, taking a morning stroll along the lush green grass of the huge yard. As you go down to the dining hall, you get the feeling that an elaborate feast has been prepared to celebrate your arrival. You go back to a different age, a different era, and become a different person. These hotels arrange for things like horseback riding in the yard, wine-tasting in the 'vintage' wine room, visits to the castle museum, grand middle-age European meals, and so on. They are not simply a hotel but are selling you an experience, a story. Even when you order room service, the waiter will be dressed like some servant from an old history book. You pay so much extra money because you are living in that story. Even if you are there for a weekend, you feel like you have come back a few hundred years. You live the story, and the story lives inside you, which is why you are ready to pay a fortune because it's not just a trip; it is your fairytale fantasy.

On the other hand, simple bed-and-breakfast places, like those found on Airbnb, are also extremely popular nowadays. You might feel that this is because they are cheap, but that's not all. People prefer to live in these places because they get a taste of the local culture and a very personal touch of hospitality from the hosts. A lot of these places offer you only the essentials like beds, pillows, and basic toiletries, and provide you with a kitchen that you can use to make your food while you stay, which might sound like too much work on a holiday, but something people nowadays like to experience while traveling. If you are staying in a nice hotel, you will get all the amenities like room service or a spa, but you will not get the local flavor of a place. Making memories is more fun when you are doing a lot on your own. You will reminisce stories to your friends like, "remember the time when we cooked lasagne on our vacation in Atlanta and almost burned it and then ordered takeout from that local diner? I can't believe they could make such an amazing cheesecake." These local places might not give you all the comforts of a fancy hotel, but they will give you a memorable time.

Heritage hotels and Airbnbs are on two opposite ends of the hospitality spectrum, but both are extremely popular and profitable because both of them sell you a different kind of experience. While heritage hotels will transfer you to an over-the-top fantasyland, Airbnbs will allow you to become a local inhabitant during your weekend getaway. The common point between these two is that both of them let you experience a story or enable you to create stories with your friends or inside your mind. You will pay a lot of money to feel like a prince or princess for a couple of days at a heritage hotel, and Airbnbs make a lot of money even though they are cheaper than normal hotels because of the local experience and personal touch that they provide to their guests.

Whenever you look at a successful business or an entrepreneur, you will find that all of them have something in common: They are not simply selling a product, but selling stories. People want an experience, even if they are out for dinner on a Friday night. You could go out to a Chinese restaurant, or visit one of those places where the chef cooks your entire meal in front of you while doing antics with their knives and woks. If you haven't been to the latter, you will probably choose that restaurant because it sounds more intriguing to you. What is so special about an ordinary Chinese restaurant? But a chef cooking your food in front of you, maybe chatting while they do it seems like a lot more fun.

This is what you need to understand: If you are someone who wants to set up their own business, a new blog, or absolutely anything that you want people to like, you will have to do more than just come up with a product or an idea and market that. You must come up with a story that your target customers or audience will relate to. Many companies sell phones, but only Apple sells iPhones. When you create an interesting story for your product, people will pay to experience that story.

Today's consumer preference is varied, but there are a lot of products to cater to their demands. Suppose your startup provides cleaning services; there are hundreds of cleaning services listed on any search engine. Why should the customer choose you? Or you have a travel blog where you regularly share pictures and detailed descriptions of all the places you have visited. There are millions of travel pages and blogs; why should the user click on yours? What can you do to stand apart from the others?

In this comprehensive guide on how to market yourself or your startup with the help of storytelling, you will find that profit comes to those who go beyond selling. You must weave a story with which a potential customer becomes enchanted. Before they know it, they have already become your customer: because they can say no to a random product, but they cannot resist the charm of a heartfelt story.

Chapter 1:

Storytelling and Business

Remember when we were children, and our parents used to take us to the doctor for a shot of a vaccine? Most children are scared of needles, and many of them would even cry when they saw the injection. But there was always a kind doctor or a nurse who would tell you stories so the process became easier. They would tell you a random story about a talking animal or how a dog went to space, and you would get distracted. Before you even know, the injection would be given, and you would get a candy bar for being a brave child.

Stories have always been an integral part of our lives. We associate sweet and fond memories with storytelling, which is why even when we are making a purchase, we are looking for stories. When you buy anything online, the first thing you do is look at the reviews. Why do you think you do it? You want to know the opinions of other people who have already purchased that product and understand how they feel. The most convincing reviews are the ones where you get stories of situations like, "When I plugged in this hair-straightener, it burst and there were flames. A small part of my curtains caught fire." You see this review and immediately decide not to buy that hair-straightener. You see another review, such as, "I gifted this watch to my brother on his birthday, and he loved it! Our dad used to have a watch like this. It has a vintage look". The website has listed all specifications of the watch, but this review made you happy because it narrates the experience of someone who had gifted it to someone who loved it. These stories resonate through us, and we make a positive or negative decision about the business or the brand. That is why storytelling is instrumental in the success of a company.

Importance of Storytelling in Business

People want to relate themselves to the business or product that they are investing in. Through trying to relate, they are looking for stories. These stories separate your brand from the rest and give your customers a reason to care. The deeper the emotional connection, the more they will be attached to your brand, making more profits for you. If you are an entrepreneur who is about to launch a startup, you must absorb the importance of storytelling for building a successful brand.

Developing Your Business

When you thought about opening your business, what was the reason behind it? Are you particularly passionate about the product? Did something happen in your personal life that gave you the impetus to start? Whatever the reason, you had a rationale behind starting your company, and people want to hear it. When you had the vision for your startup, you must have had a problem in your mind that you were venturing to solve. Share that problem with your customers through a relatable story with which they can connect. When you are relating a problem to people, they make themselves a part of that problem, a character in that story, helping build trust and the development of business.

Gives You the Edge

When you are telling a good story, your customers will be personally attached to your brand, creating brand loyalty and giving you a competitive advantage over your business rivals. There are so many brands for every product in today's market, which makes it extremely important to have something unique in your marketing strategy that will enable you to stand out; a good story behind your brand will help you achieve that. Random items are sold for thousands of dollars on eBay because of all the touching testimonials written with them, raising the auction price, earning the seller a huge profit.

Creating a Solid Marketing Strategy

Many entrepreneurs have grand ideas about what their brand should represent and what they wish to convey to the world. However, when it comes to implementation, it becomes hollow and ambiguous because the ideas are scattered and lack direction. It helps to have a story, through which the company will create its visions and missions. When a marketing strategy is built under the umbrella of a story, the strategy becomes clear and concrete; every piece will have a purpose and be in tune with the overall objectivity of your company. If you want to convey the intent of your brand, do so through a story so that you can retain your customers' attention.

Create an Efficient Workforce

The success of a business does not only depend on the customers but the people who are working there. Your employees are the backbone of all activities and it is very important to keep them motivated to ensure the success of the business. Storytelling helps you motivate your employees, makes them realize that they are a part of something bigger, and that this is more than a job. The weekly paycheck is not enough to keep morale high at all times, which is why you need to give them a story in which to believe. When you share stories about your struggle with your employees, they will empathize with you and may also come forward to share their struggles and develop a bond that goes beyond the employer-employee relationship.

Companies today need a greater sense of responsibility while marketing their products. People, especially millennials, prefer companies that are doing something for the society and environment, only customer-oriented marketing is not enough. You have to care about social issues if you want your customers to like you and your brand. Inform your customers with the help of a good story about how you are being sustainable and why you stand out from other brands.

When telling a story to promote your company, remember to include real people and real situations. Customers care about people, which is what will affect their decisions about your brand. They want to know that the marketing messages are not merely messages and that you thrive to create an inclusive environment inside your organization. Providing a sneak-peak inside your company and what it is like working for you will create involvement. Show your customers what an average working day looks like inside your company. Show them your workspace, your cafeteria, and your break-room. Simply saying that your company is a "fun place" to work will not resonate with the customers. They need examples, and they need to see your employees enjoying what they do, that is how they will be convinced that your products are indeed made with love. Once you show your research team having fun while creating the next product, the customers will know that talented people are giving their best to produce something extraordinary. For a long time, companies thought that their trade and production process must be a secret and that is how they can stay on top of the game. But now, providing a little peek into your affairs will make you more popular with your customers, they will feel that they are a part of your company, and brand loyalty will be formed. Remember, the secret ingredient is your story and nothing else.

A few years ago, Google produced a short advertisement showing how their search engine helps people find the rarest of things, including long-lost friends and neighborhoods. It was a tear-jerking ride about two separated friends, who are now older men, who found each other years later with the help of Google. This story was remarkable because it was relatable to the millions of people across the world who have been separated from their loved ones because of political partitions, and this advertisement paid homage to all such people and their stories. Google is so much bigger than just a search engine, and it stands apart from all its competitors for these reasons.

Why Some Stories are Remembered

Storytelling is an art that can be used to boost the performance of your company. Once you get the hang of it, you will understand why certain brands are more popular than others. The success of your brand will depend on how well you can narrate your story to your customers. People have very short attention spans, and it is difficult to keep someone captivated unless you have something interesting to say. When you are watching a video on YouTube with an advertisement before the main video, it annoys you, and you skip it the moment those mandatory ten or fifteen seconds are over. But, if the advertisement is captivating or relevant to you, you might just end up watching the whole thing; that is good advertising and better storytelling because that brand managed to capture your attention even when you are not obligated to watch it.

We will meet so many people in our lives and forget about most of them, but we remember the stories they told us. If you are coming up with something new, a business, blog, or anything, create a remarkable story behind your product. I follow a food blog page on Instagram, and in every recipe video, you can see the person's pet dog accompanying them in all the steps. For example, the dog might go and fetch a towel, or he might simply sit and wag his tail, adding a unique and compelling aspect because the dog is absolutely adorable. I found it a bit strange, so I dug a little deeper into the profile, and one of their first posts revealed that the page author divulged that they had to take up cooking when their mom passed away a couple of years back. They lived near their mom's place, and they never had to cook because she sent food almost every day, until after her death when they had to learn for themselves, soon finding their passion. When they thought they had become good at it, they decided to open a food blog, sharing videos of all the recipes they tried. During this rough phase, while grieving the death of their mother, it was their dog who never left their side. During all those recipe fails and breakdowns amidst cooking, it was the dog who always consoled them, which is why they decided it would only be appropriate that the dog was a part of every video. That is how the entire gimmick started, and now that page has more than one hundred thousand followers across all social media platforms. This is such a beautiful story behind marketing a product; it is genuine, and people relate to it because the death of a loved one and unconditional love from their dogs is something a lot of us have experienced.

Ever since the hit of the Covid-19 Pandemic, people all across the world have started making recipe videos and uploading them on social media platforms. How many of them gain that kind of popularity, though? They are not popular because they are basic and have nothing unique about them. In short, they lack a story. People know how to make lasagne, you need to add some extra ingredients to make yours special. That extra ingredient comes from a good story, that is what people find appealing. Whether you are launching a startup or a simple blog, to be successful, you need to build your entire branding on a good story.

How to Tell the Story of Your Product

When you are thinking about marketing your product through storytelling, you have to remember to go all in. There must be depth in your stories. Otherwise, it can come off as fake. It is okay if your stories are not perfect because people relate to imperfections; try to be as personal as you can and touch the hearts of your customers. While you have to woo your customers, be careful not to be overcome by your own emotions. After all, you are promoting your product or business and not simply telling a story in your family gathering. Here are a few tips that can help you to understand how to create a story that promotes your product.

Step 1: Identify the Protagonist

The first step for creating any story is to identify the hero. When promoting your business, the protagonist of your story can be your customer, employee, partner, investor, or product. You can also be the protagonist of your story. It is important to choose a protagonist with whom your customers will relate because you can only create a successful story when your customers think that the protagonist's problem is their problem. The hero must invoke empathy from the customers.

Step 2: Show the Problem

Once the protagonist is introduced, you have to bring their problems into the spotlight and put them in a vulnerable position so the customers can feel their pain, which is where the emotions come into play. You have to showcase your protagonist as someone who is in a tight situation, from which it is extremely difficult to remove themselves. This is how you can try to cue in the necessity of your product without being explicit; just put the problem on the table, and the customer's mind will automatically wander into thoughts about how the poor thing comes out of this fix.

Step 3: Identify the Guide Who Can Lead Them to the Solution

This step can become a bit tricky because when you are telling a story about promoting your product, you cannot be too direct. The guide can be someone the protagonist knows, like their friend or relative, or you can allow the audience to think the protagonist is being guided by their conscience. For example, if you are launching a startup selling plant-based meats, introducing a guide can be something like this: "So many poor animals are dying because they are used as meat, it breaks my heart. I know one person cannot make a difference, but I wonder what steps I can take to reduce the amount a little bit?"

Step 4: Introduce a Solution

Once the guide has directed them towards the solution, the next natural step is to introduce the actual solution in the story. You must remember that you are simply telling a story to educate and enlighten your protagonist about the solutions to the struggles they are facing. You are not selling a product. You have to let the customer decide that the product you are offering is the most natural solution to their problems and handle this step very delicately because you cannot dictate to the customer that your product is the way out.

Step 5: Show How the Solution Really Solves All Problems

This is the final step where you show that the proposed solution is, in fact, the best alternative to the struggles the customer is facing. The story concludes, and the customer is left with a sense of satisfaction that their problems are solved. The objective is to make the customer feel they are in charge and under no obligation to buy anything, and that it is their choice that they chose this particular brand which happened to put an end to their struggles.

While following these steps can help you create a great story for your startup, you must also remember that these are only for your guidance. There are a million ways to tell a story, and you know best what makes your product work. The main point of a story is to be creative, so you can choose a million options to communicate your idea. The important thing to remember here is that your customers want a story they want to hear and not a story you want to tell. You are telling a story not to share your personal feelings but subtly communicate the benefits of your products and satisfy your customers.

Why Storytelling is Such a Powerful Communication Strategy

As I said, people want more than just your product. Telling a story allows them to trust you and count on you. When you are telling a story, the customers are listening to you and feeling with you. If you simply give a presentation about the products your company offers, the feeling of empathy is missing, the customer is bored, and they have already decided they do not want to buy from you. You can treat your customers like children, who can be lured by flashy pictures and interesting stories and can communicate your idea a hundred times better by doing so. Facts and figures are not always appealing to customers. Imagine you have gone to buy a television with a salesperson who goes on and on about the sales figures of a particular television model and how successful the projection reports are. You listen to all that and nod your head, but you are distracted because you are not interested in these figures. You dream about how the television will look in your living room and how you can watch movies and matches with your family over the weekend, and how the Super Bowl will become more fun to watch with a big TV like this. Whenever you think about buying something, your mind instantly wanders off to imaginary situations with that product. Like while buying a dress, you will imagine how you will look in it. Your imagination lets you create an opinion about the dress even before you try it on. If a brand eases this process of imagination for you through stories and scenarios, the selling points of that brand are communicated to you in a better way. Communication is much more efficient when the subject comes to you in the form of a story, which is why the new apps where kids can learn basic Mathematics, English, and other subjects are so popular. A teacher can explain to the kids how two plus two makes four, but when they are using the app where they can put two oranges and two apples in a basket, it becomes easier for them to remember that the basket has four fruits. Just listening to a teacher is not particularly entertaining for a child, whereas when they are playing a game, they are having fun. Whenever there is the presence of an emotion, we tend to remember things better. Memory becomes stronger whenever there is a strong feeling attached to it, which is why you still remember how your mom scolded you for breaking something when you were ten years old. You felt bad, and that is why the memory has lingered, just as the memory would linger after an event that made you feel good.

The process of communication starts with the encoding of a message by the sender and finally ends with decoding the same message by the receiver. This process might sound technical to you, but it's simple. Stories help the process of communication by making it efficient. When you are trying to communicate the benefits of using your product through a story, you are encoding a subtle message which reaches your customer as an emotional appeal and not as a marketing strategy. Stories help to put a human factor in your marketing strategy and make the customers believe in your product while communicating the essence of a brand in a more natural way, rather than imposing it on the customers.

There is no need to feel that you have to use storytelling only for the larger canvas. It is efficient on which to base your entire marketing strategy, but storytelling can come in handy during your day-to-day operations as well.

- Presentations: When you are making a presentation, it is a good idea to make use of storytelling. Presentations are usually brief, meaning you get a shorter period of time to communicate yourself. Make sure your story is short and hits the main points while also including facts and figures. An unnecessarily long story might deviate your customer from the main focus of the presentation.

- Introducing your product or company to a new client: When you are visiting a potential client for the first time, you might want to use a "who am I" story in which you will demonstrate how and why you came up with the business and what you can offer to the customer. Wrap all the information inside a beautifully narrated story and you will be good to go.

Stories help you to share your values about your company to your potential customers. Suppose you own a line of cosmetic products; when you promote your products to people, you mention that these products are cruelty-free which means that none of these products are tested on animals. You can choose to impart this information with the help of a story about how you grew up on a farm and how attached you are to animals, and that you would never start a company that hurts animals for testing products. Your target audience will empathize with you because of the personal experience you just shared and how that determines the future plans of the company. You project yourself as a brand that is kind and environmentally sustainable, which is what we mean by brand storytelling. The simple story about you growing up on a farm gives your customers a sneak peek into what your operations look like and what your values are as a company. Small story, but it goes a long way in promoting a healthy image of your brand.

Chapter 2:

Brand Storytelling

When you think of the brand Disney, what is the first thing that comes to your mind? Is it the movies, the merchandise, or the theme park? It is difficult to pinpoint anything in particular when it comes to Disney. Children love to watch Disney movies, whether it is a fairytale or Pixar, a whole generation of teenagers and adults are obsessed with the entire Marvel Cinematic Universe, and children and their parents all love to go to Disneyland. When you think of Disney, your face brightens up with a smile because it is not just a brand. Parents can blindly trust their children to watch a Disney movie because there is nothing inappropriate and they get to learn about a number of family values. My seven-year-old nephew's favorite superhero is a woman called Captain Marvel, which is impressive given that women superheroes were never quite popular back in the old days. You'll find news of so many couples who proposed to their partners in Disneyland. My point is, Disney is not just a theme park or a production house that produces high-budget superhero movies. It speaks about social issues, ideal characters who are also imperfect in their own ways. Disney uses its power of storytelling to communicate what they stand for as a brand.

What is Brand Storytelling?

Brand Storytelling involves using a narrative to convey the business objectives of a company. Essentially, you are letting your customers know what you stand for with the help of a story. There is no direct selling involved, just a simple indication of why your brand is different and what values you wish to impart. Disney might have started off as a cartoon and comics, but over the years they have evolved into a bigger brand by letting people know their purpose. Nowadays, every Disney movie has a deep social message embedded in them and their modern takes on the classic fairy tales distinguish them from others. For example, they remade Aladdin so that, in the end, Jasmine becomes the Sultan because she was the worthy queen. When they made Captain America, they portrayed him as the weak boy from Brooklyn who stood up for himself even before he took the serum and became strong. Disney shows people that they stand for equality, inclusivity, and a positive approach. All this is achieved with the help of storytelling; they have built the foundation of their brand with the help of stories, and look how profitable they have become.

It is impossible to convey your mission to your customers without storytelling, which is why Brand Storytelling is now the most successful marketing strategy today. By tapping the universal human love for stories, brands can create deeper connections with their customers. Once the customers are clear about your purpose, they will see you as more than just another brand selling products. They will relate to the brand and form personal attachments, which is the first step towards creating brand loyalty. It is important to remember that buying is often an emotional decision rather than a practical one, and storytelling often adds fuel to this emotional process.

Brand Storytelling Framework

Brand storytelling is not some made-up bedtime story that you can tell your kids to make them fall asleep. While it is important to invoke the emotions of the customer, you have to do that carefully and schematically. In order to do that, you have to be organized and frame your story in a smart way. Remember, customers have a million choices and if you want them to choose you, your story should really stand out. Different brands will have different stories, so there is no standard formula for storytelling. However, there are a few basic factors that need consideration while you're framing a story for your brand.

Who are You?

Before you tell your story to your customers, ask yourself who you are. How did this startup come into existence? If it was you who set it up, then you should isolate the events that led you to form this company. Structured brand storytelling is a relatively new concept, and if your company was formed by your father or someone from the previous generation, it might be a good idea to do a quick refresher on the foundations of the company. You should also list what kind of employees work under you and whether there is anything remarkable about your recruitment process.

What Are Your Products?

The next factor to be considered while framing your brand story is your product. What is it that you are offering your customers? Is it a product or a service? You must have seen the legendary ways in which Steve Jobs always introduced his new products: Be it the Mac or the iPhone, he would narrate such an amazing story that your focus would completely shift from the fact that he is selling something. While you are focussing on the kind of products or services that you offer, you have to factor in what kind of interactions these products will create with the customers.

Who Are Your Target Customers?

When you are trying to tell a story about your brand, you have to identify your target audience. When Nike comes up with a new item of sportswear, their target audience is mostly the young fitness freaks. When Barbie comes up with a new model of their doll, their target audience is children under age 12 and their parents who will be buying the doll for them. The two stories are going to be different because the people hearing the stories are different. It is essential to determine who your customers will be to customize your story accordingly.

What Are Your Ultimate Objectives?

This one will need a lot of consideration from you. If you are the founder of your company, you must have a clear idea about its long-term plans and goals. Do you want to create an international market for your brand? Or do you plan towards overall economic development by providing employment to all sections of the society as your company grows? When you figure out the bigger goal, it is easier to frame your story based on those goals. Your bigger future plans let you create an atmosphere of suspense that intrigues your customers.

What is the Process?

You might feel that the customers do not want to know the boring production process behind the end product, but you are absolutely mistaken. People will be interested in anything if you can tell the story properly, and exposing your production process is a good way to connect better with your customers. A lot of big restaurants these days organize behind-the-scenes actions where they take a journalist on a tour of their kitchen, and the chefs show how they prepare the popular delicacies and what goes into their favorite dish. There used to be a lot of secrecy amongst restaurants because they did not want anybody to imitate their signature items, but once they started showing the entire process, people were even more awed by the effort it takes to create the dish.

If you are a small entrepreneur, all this talk about structured storytelling might intimidate you. So let me tell you a story so that you can understand storytelling better: There was an old lady in our neighborhood who used to sell these amazing sauces and pickled meats. She mostly did it out of passion and distributed them to those who lived nearby. Everyone paid her, although she never asked for any money. You can't technically call it a business, but she kept on selling for years. A few years ago, I went home for the holidays. I had to pick up some toiletries, so I went to the local store. I was surprised to see a whole counter of "Grandma's Sauces & Pickles," with the picture of that old lady. The whole counter was decorated with pictures showing how the sauce was made and why it is 100% organic and safe, as well as cute pop-outs that showed testimonials of all the local people who have used these products for a long time. I even saw a smiling picture of my mom, who highly recommended this lady's product because of its aroma and freshness. I was taken aback because I never knew the old lady had made such a name for her products. I picked up two bottles of sauce and pickled meat, and when I was at the check-out, the billing guy told me that these sauces were the most popular in every shop within a fifty-mile radius. I came back home and asked my mom about the phenomenal success of our childhood sauce-lady and she informed me that it was her grandson who had built the business. He came to all the houses in the neighborhood and asked their opinions on the sauce, and hired professional videographers to shoot a detailed video of the entire "production process," which is basically grandma making the sauce in her yard. He brilliantly marketed the product, and now it is a popular choice in many local stores. Mom said he has also opened pages on various social media platforms where he posts daily updates about the business.

So, you see, storytelling does not pertain to big corporations and startups; you can use the power of a good story in any business, you simply need to visualize how you want the customers to see your brand. Grandma's Sauces & Pickles might not be an international brand yet, but it is doing pretty good for something that she basically gave out for free. I checked out their social media pages, and they are doing a brilliant job there as well. Just the other day they posted updates about going to their farm nearby and picking out the tomatoes, continuously updating throughout the day. It started with them waking up early because they had a "surprise" plan, took a three-hour drive, and finally reached their destination. The viewers who are following them are anticipating what they are doing and where they are going. All of us check our phones a million times in a day, each time their followers are scrolling and swiping, they are seeing an update from them. They are telling the story of how they select the best tomatoes and how they are handpicked to be made into the sauce. Just imagine, you are at work replying to emails and each time you open Instagram, you are waiting for their next update. Did they pick the tomatoes yet? How many did they pick? Are they going to make a salad from these for their lunch? A simple trick of storytelling is keeping you hooked.

How Can You Make Your Brand Story Resonate With Your Customers?

Making yourself memorable is not an easy task, which is why even brands with potential are forgotten. If you want your customers to remember you, you have to maintain a constant presence everywhere, including TV, radio commercials, or even simple social media posts. People make a big mistake by thinking that the job ends after developing the content. The main aspect to successful brand storytelling is promoting your story in every possible way. You can create fancy stories about your brand and mission, but they would go unnoticed unless you make them visible in the right places and to the right people. It helps if you create an appropriate buyer persona for your product which means identifying your main customers.

Making yourself visible is an important aspect of marketing your brand, you can take the example of the people from Grandma's Sauces & Pickles since they have created their personal brand with the help of simple stories. When you are telling the story of your brand, it is important to keep it as simple as possible. Brand stories are basically advertisements, and nobody likes an awkwardly long commercial. You should create a simple theme and develop multiple stories around it, stories that should be constantly visible everywhere. A simple story with a powerful message resonates the most with any kind of audience.

Using social media is a good and inexpensive option to make these series of stories visible to your potential customers. Create a brand story that will be continuously shared by all the people associated with your brand, like your employees, management, and so on. You can also ask happy customers to share these stories on their social media platforms to increase their reach. The key is to share these stories across every available platform to reach a maximum number of people. If you keep doing this long enough, your stories will become an integral part of your brand.

If you want to have a lasting impact on your customers, create a product persona, meaning that you need to humanize your product. If your product was a human being, how would you describe its nature to your audience? For example, if the product is KFC's fried chicken, what kind of a person would it be? In my personal opinion, the fried chicken is like the girl-next-door, loved by everyone and perfectly suited for all occasions, but she also likes to have fun and boasts of having a little zing in her character. If it feels stupid to you, think again because this is a fun way of reaching your customers and telling a story without actually stuffing the product on the customer's plate.

Another effective way to make your customers remember you is by engaging them in your stories and campaigns. You will find big brands and influencers asking their audience to share their personal stories, the best stories winning some prizes. By asking your audience to engage in your storytelling process, you are creating a deep bond with them, and making them feel validated and important. When they see their personal story shared by a popular brand, it makes the brand and the story more human. Brands like Dove have always shifted their focus from the magazine standards of beauty to stories of real women having real problems. Recently, world-famous lingerie brand Victoria's Secret replaced their age-old models with successful women from different walks of life. Women all over the world complained that these models, also called 'angel's, portrayed unrealistic standards of beauty and body measurements. They said that no real woman looked like those models and thus they could not relate to the brand, which is why Victoria's Secret decided to change their marketing strategy and make more realistic women their models. People are not looking for something they can never achieve, that is not how marketing works anymore. Now, people are looking for relatable stories and characters who speak to them, they are trying to find themselves within these stories. The success of a brand depends on how they can make their audience feel comfortable with their stories and make them a part of it.

Examples of Successful Brand Storytelling

It is becoming increasingly popular among brands to use the power of storytelling to promote themselves. In 2015, Ikea Singapore launched a campaign called "Improve Your Private Life." This campaign showed a "shelf-help guru" who would ask potential Ikea customers to improve their bedrooms and bathrooms by discovering new shelves and furniture, and was particularly successful because of its humorous tone and puns. Ikea was bold enough to get up-close and personal with the customer by venturing inside the most private parts of their homes. They continued this campaign via Facebook where people could ask their shelf-help guru about ways to improve the decor in their homes; every person would get a reply in the form of a funny comment, and a link directing them to a specific product from Ikea. This might seem like a simple technique, but it was widely appreciated by the people. Ikea also declared to reward a lucky winner a gift card worth $50, which further increased the excitement among people.

Huggies, the diaper brand, faced stiff competition from market leader Pampers and thought about putting some unique storytelling into their marketing campaign. They made it as simple as they could and stole their story theme from their own title. In Canada, they launched a campaign highlighting the need for direct skin contact for babies, meaning that babies have a physical need to be hugged, and Huggies is there to make sure that happens all the time. Another objective of this campaign was to show that Canadian hospitals had volunteers who would hug babies whenever they needed direct skin contact—a killer storytelling strategy because they were showing the importance of hugging babies. Could it really get any more convincing?

There are hundreds of examples of successful brand storytelling and how they have impacted the customers. One more is how IBM used their Artificial Intelligence Watson to do a social awareness campaign on melanoma in Australian people. They used their information and analytics to promote Watson while shedding light on a very serious health issue. Brand storytelling is not a new concept, it has been there for ages. Schlitz beer used the technique of showing their entire production process in their advertisement to prove the purity of their beer. It was during the early 1900s and all beer brands wanted to portray their product as the purest, but Schlitz took it to the next level by taking their customers on a tour of their factory through their advertisement. They showed the special cooling mechanism, sterilizing of the bottles, and double-cleansing every piece of equipment, which ensured the purity of the end product. Sales numbers increased rapidly because customers saw that Schlitz was a genuinely pure brand of beer.

It is beyond arguments that storytelling is always a more effective way of promoting a brand in comparison to other methods. Direct facts and figures do not stay with the customers, but a deeper connection with the things they will be putting their money into does. This is why all successful brands resort to telling a good story when promoting themselves.

Why Brand Storytelling is the Future of Marketing

We have surrounded ourselves with too many gadgets which have made our lives mechanical. Ever since the Covid-19 pandemic, people all across the world have been locked down in the isolation of their homes. Loneliness has become more intense and it is making us crave some human emotions and love. We try to compensate for the death of emotions in our lives by looking for brands and products that seem comforting to us., which is why brand storytelling has become the most popular marketing strategy, and it will remain so for a long time to come.

Stories make brands distinct and separate from others. In this sea of brands and marketing gimmicks, it is difficult to stand out. You might think of yourself as a part of the crowd, but you are unique and so are your stories. People want to hear your stories because that is what makes your brand different from the rest. It might be something really simple, but heartfelt emotions are much better than typical and cosmetic advertisements. The facts and figures are good for your financial statements, but does your regular customer relate to it? You could tell them a story about how you came up with the company logo while taking a walk on the beach rather than telling them how much you paid to buy the rights for that logo.

When promoting a product through storytelling, you are not gaining customers, you are building a tribe. In the initial days of any company, your finances might not always be stable, but if you are able to build a solid customer base, you will gain loyal advocates for life. You need to offer something greater than a product or service, achieved with the help of storytelling. Once you tell them your stories, they will believe in you and start buying from you. Those days are gone when salespersons could make false claims and get away with them. Today's customers are much more informed and aware, and can differentiate the genuine from the fake, which is why the best option is to stay real.

Your customers want you to get personal with them, which is why the Ikea campaign was so successful. The barriers are breaking when it comes to personal conversations; customers like to be asked difficult questions. Uncomfortable scenarios don't make the customers uneasy but feel that as a brand you have the guts to approach the difficult topics. It is no longer the age where you need to keep all your opinions to yourself and be politically correct. When you give an opinion, your customers will understand your take on sensitive issues and take a part in that. Even if some of them disagree, they will applaud you for sharing your opinion. People know how difficult it can be for brands to express opinions, and if you do so, your customers will respect you.

If you are about to set up a new business, it is important to determine your brand positioning beforehand. Your methods of storytelling will depend on what kind of a brand you want yourself to be. Delving into the personal lives of your customers through interactive stories and engagements will enable you to achieve specialization in your industry. You will be able to determine your niche market once you know what your customers need.

Suppose your startup deals with pet supplies: You sell toys, treats, pet food, collars harnesses, and things like that. You are thinking of expanding your business, but are not sure what new to bring to the table because you already sell everything that a standard pet store has. Even medical care is out of consideration because your store is connected to a vet clinic. What can you do? This situation is where storytelling will come to your aid. You can start a social media campaign, where you ask all your followers to share stories about their pets and that one thing which they would want their pets to have. To attract more people to the campaign, you can ask the followers to send in their entries with a cute picture of their pet, and a few selected people will get a pack of treats delivered to them. To increase engagement even more, you can offer freebies to every person who sends in an entry.

In America, every other household has pets, especially dogs. Dogs make the best pets, but they are pretty high-maintenance and suffer from separation anxiety, feeling scared when they are left alone, and It is not possible for people to always stay with them. Once you get all the entries, people will share their stories with you and you may find out that the most common thing that all people want for their pets is to prevent them from separation anxiety when the owners are not at home. The more stories you get, the more you understand the pain of your customers, helping you to come up with products like indoor activities for your pet, or interactive cameras that dispense treats and keep the pets entertained. You can continue this storytelling campaign when you are introducing your new product and let the customers know that you hear them and their stories have inspired you to come up with a new line of products. The customers will feel validated and will buy from you because you directly addressed their concerns and came up with a new solution.

The thing about storytelling is that it's not just for customers. The beauty of this modern approach to marketing is that these stories help you come up with new ideas and lead to market specialization. Stories help you identify your customers' concerns, and which concerns are not being addressed. Smells like an untapped profitable niche, doesn't it?

Chapter 3:

Selecting Your Niche Through Storytelling

Suppose you want to start your own company or launch a startup: You have worked at a company that manufactures umbrellas and backpacks for over a decade, and you know everything there is to know about these products. With your varied experience and expertise, you decide to start your own backpack company. You know all the vendors, and your time at the company has taught you what the possible mistakes that affect sales might be. You start your business and it's going pretty well because backpacks are always in demand. You offer almost every variety of backpacks because you know that customer demands are varied, and you have to have a diversified product line to keep all your customers satisfied.

All of this seems fine, but what extra efforts are you taking to make your company stand apart? There are many companies selling backpacks, and you are not even amongst the big ones, so why should people choose you? What is unique about your brand? Today, people are spoiled with so many choices that you will be very easily overlooked if you don't have that oomph factor in your brand. How do you identify the factor that will set you apart?

Take some help from your old friend named storytelling. Ask around, and do some research about what people want when they are buying a backpack. Is it more space, more compartments, or another dedicated place for a second water bottle? Ask people randomly, not as a seller, and you will get your feedback. Once you have conducted thorough and mindful research, you will find some peculiar specifications that your customers might be asking for in their backpacks. Suppose your company is located in one of the hilly states, so you are more likely to find people who are interested in hiking. You can customize your backpacks especially for these hikers. Your company can start specializing in backpacks for hikers, which is a particularly specialized market, and you will cater to a very specific customer base, known as a niche.

You must remember that niches don't necessarily exist, but are created. What I mean is, there is no active market of backpacks for hikers, this is just something sellers came up with during interactions with people. Once again, storytelling saves the day. Suppose you had gone on a hike yourself and met a few fellow hikers on the way: One of them tore their backpacks while climbing up, and you overheard them complaining about how backpacks are not strong enough to endure elaborate hikes. Niches are identified by research and interactions with people and their stories. A niche market is basically a specialized, smaller segment of an already existing market, but offers specific goods or services that address a unique demand that sellers in the larger market are overlooking. A niche market helps you to develop a loyal customer base because you are looking after a very specific demand otherwise overlooked by the bigger sellers of the market.

How to Determine Your Niche Market

The key to finding your niche market is conducting an in-depth examination of your customers, demographics, and many other socio-economic factors. The most common factors that can be used to define your niche market are values, customer taste and preference, price and quality of the product, and income of the customer. For example, in a small industrial town, where most people belong to a middle-income bracket, it might not be a good idea to introduce specialized and ridiculously high-priced products. Careful interaction with your customer base will help you to figure out what your niche market can be.

Determine What You are Good at

While selecting your niche, it is important to conduct a SWOT analysis of yourself. Try to figure out what drives you the most, what you are passionate about because niches are highly specialized markets, and it is essential that you believe in your product. Dig deeper into yourself, ask yourself who are the people you want to connect with. Are there any specific problems in your mind that you wish to solve? Once you have narrowed down your problem areas, you can ask yourself whether you will be able to provide better solutions to those problems than your competitors.

Research Your Industry and Customer Base

Whatever industry in which you are operating, there must be some unexplored area in it. Try to find out which areas of your specific industry have not yet been touched by your competitors. Once you find that, you have to determine the profitability of that area; maybe those markets are untapped for a reason. Search for any previous competition within that niche, and if the competitors had to shut down operations, look into the reasons why.

Another effective tip for discovering new niches is to search for various product categories on popular shopping sites, like Amazon, where you will find hundreds of categories. Suppose your company produces jackets, and you want to find out whether there is scope for discovering a new niche market: You look through Amazon and see the various categories under Jackets and might find something unique, like a quilted lightweight jacket, and search under that category. If you find there are many results under that category, this niche has already been explored. If you find few results without any ratings or reviews, then people are most likely not buying these jackets. If you find a few products with good ratings and reviews, there may be a possibility of discovering a niche market here.

You have to know your customer base and what they want. For example, People living in cities and towns by the beach will have a larger demand for beach accessories and swimwear. You have to factor in demographics while you are searching for your niche. Audience engagement and storytelling will play a pivotal role in getting to know your specific customer base.

Test and Adjust Accordingly

It is an unrealistic expectation that your selected niche will be super successful right from the beginning, it is perfectly possible that your niche market failed to attract the consumer attention that you thought it would. No reason to get bummed out, simply analyze what went wrong and adjust your niche accordingly. You need to analyze whether the fault was in the marketing strategy or the selection of the niche. It may be possible that your niche selection was right, but you failed to reach the correct target audience. You should mix and match various other marketing techniques and see whether you get your desired response.

Successful Examples of Niche Marketing

Veganism is the newest vogue in health and dieting right now. It has reached the height of its popularity, with many brands trying to come up with plant-based alternatives to regular non-vegetarian foods. Just as people were starting to learn about veganism without many options for vegan foods, Divvies came up with cookies and other sweet products, completely vegan and free of nuts. A million brands are selling these sweet products, but marking them as vegan made the difference for Divvies because that was an unexplored area in the sweet foods market. Their vegan cookies and cupcakes gave vegans the encouragement and satisfaction that they will not have to deprive themselves of anything because of their choice.

Another good option to identify your niche is to focus on any kind of minority communities, which is what Lefty's: The Left Hand Store did. Most people around the world are right-handed, and common appliances are made according to them, leaving the left-handed people of the world at a great inconvenience. Lefty's understood their problems and opened a store where they sold products made exclusively for left-handed people, including common items like scissors, kitchen gloves, and so on. Just try to use your regular pair of scissors with your left hand. Feels weird and uncomfortable, doesn't it? Lefty's identified a very specific niche market and designed their products for very specific customers.

Using Storytelling to Define Your Profitable Niche

All this talk about niches must have got you thinking, what has it got to do with storytelling? Isn't this all technical marketing jargon? Yes, it is, but it has everything to do with storytelling. The whole point of defining a niche is to find out what people want. It is about looking for the specific tastes and preferences of your target audience. How do you expect to find that if you are not listening to the stories of your customers? Your customers will most likely not just come to you and tell you that they have very specific demands relating to a product they use.

Due to the Covid-19 Pandemic, people have been locked up in their homes for the last year, so you decide to launch a startup that will manufacture home workstation units: Since most people are now working from home, they are feeling the need to have a proper workstation where they can set up their laptops and cameras so that it becomes easier to attend virtual meetings. Your startup has identified a specific demand within the furniture industry, and it looks like you have found your niche market. So, you start publicizing your startup on all social media platforms, and you get a pretty good response. Even before the operations started, you had already bagged pre-orders from quite a few people and are happy because it looks like you're going to be making a lot of money. A few months later, disappointment sets in as sales are not as high as you expected. After the initial set of pre-orders, you got a few more in the next couple of months, but after that, it seems you have hit a complete slump. What could possibly be the reason?

You are at a crossroads; you can either let this initial failure get to you, or you can sit and assess what went wrong. The ladder is always advisable if you wish to develop a successful business. So how do you start analyzing your mistakes? Enquire from your customers. There is no need to feel that if you show your failure to your customers, they will judge you. Today, customers want to feel more connected to the brands and want to understand them better. Go to all your social media pages and ask your customers what went wrong. Ask them to share stories about how your workstations are fitting in or not fitting in with your home and new working conditions. You will be amazed how these stories will help you in identifying your mistakes. Maybe you will find a lot of people commenting that your home workstation units are too big, and many people don't have such big houses to accommodate them. Many others might comment that they prefer to sit on the bed while working from home, which is why they find such big units useless. These insights will help you to realize that maybe your units need to be resized to fit into small or medium-sized houses. Moreover, you get to know that if someone is sitting on the bed and working throughout the day, they are bound to face problems in keeping the laptop. You can start producing smaller tables which can be kept on the bed to keep their laptops and work. When more people share more stories, you can define your niche more efficiently. You will get to know that people are having back problems due to sitting with bad posture throughout the day while working from home., you can add comfortable chairs in your workstation unit or pillows that provide lumbar support. The more stories you hear, the more you will be able to achieve perfection within your niche.

In marketing, storytelling works both ways. You can create a story for your brand, or you can ask your customers to share their stories to help you to identify your niche. Using storytelling to search for your niche can be an effective way to communicate your values to your potential customers. Once you gather your research about the possible unexplored areas of consumer demand, you can use stories to reach your customers, helping you to stay true to your brand value and make connections. As an entrepreneur, you can follow these steps to use storytelling in becoming an expert in your niche:

Develop Your Social Media Voice

Social media is a great way to showcase your values and get to know your customers better. When a popular brand makes a post on social media, you will find there are thousands of comments. While a lot of those comments don't make much sense, if you look through them closely, you will find many people sharing important and heartfelt information that might be beneficial in the search for a niche. Many brands create a unique internet voice for themselves that may be entirely positive or even a bit sassy. For example, Brooklinen updated a post in the form of an email sent by a digital marketing intern about an upcoming sale. It seemed that email was a part of personal correspondence, and it was put up on social media as a mistake. While the entire social media was buzzing about how Brooklinen has made a terrible mistake, they upload subsequent posts where they make fun of the intern in a cute positive way, then announcing they are having a big sale. It was a great example of how a little storytelling helped them create a tremendous marketing strategy. Their humorous social media voice showcased them as a funny and inclusive brand that does not penalize their interns for mistakes.

Get Direct Feedback

As I keep saying, finding your niche means finding an area of specialization in an already established market, and the best way to do that is by asking your customers directly what they want. While there are many examples of how customer feedback helps in creating a niche market, one that particularly stands out is that of PinkCab. While companies like Uber provide pickup and drop services at all times of the day, at night, many women feel unsafe to use Uber. Justifiably, because of all the harassment reports about Uber drivers. Although Uber has female drivers, their algorithm does not allow you to select a driver of your choice, which is where PinkCabs identified and found its niche market. When the news of sexual harassment by male drivers was peaking, PinkCab introduced a unique feature that allowed a woman to choose a reliable woman driver for her late-night pickup or mid-day drop-off. The stories about women feeling scared in Uber rides made an impact, and PinkCab used this opportunity to provide a service and create a safe space for all women.

Create A Value Proposition

A value proposition is something that uniquely separates you from your competitors. In order to develop a value proposition statement, you have to have in-depth knowledge about your market and customers. Value proposition might seem like a slogan, but it is deeper than that. It stands for the bigger values, what you stand for, which gives you the competitive edge. A value proposition statement will include a detailed analysis of your customers and their needs, wants, and fears.

The founders of Slack initially started off developing a game. They were hopeful about that game but people did not seem to accept it. That's when Slack was born, as a communication platform for all teammates where information would easily be accessible. Slack has a brilliant value proposition where they focus on being 'pleasant'. It is a focused chatroom and a faster means of communication than email. As more people wanted to use a platform that felt like a private place for their work community, Slack started adding more features that enhanced its pleasantness.

How Storytelling Helps Brand Positioning

With the widespread availability of books in online stores and the popularity of e-books, physical bookstores have suffered losses and a decline in customers. Most people now like to invest in a kindle rather than stacking up loads of books in an attempt to be sustainable and eco-friendly. Almost all bookstores took this paradigm shift to the heart and started defensive marketing techniques highlighting why bookstores are important. But not Powell's Books. Powell's is one of the biggest independent bookstores in the USA, and they deal in both new and used books. However, instead of despising the internet, they embraced it and made great use of it. Through social media engagements and hashtags, they kept their brand alive in the minds of their customers. They regularly organize online book discussions along with sponsored events and giveaways. Audience engagement has enabled them to be perceived as a modern brand and does not shy away from embracing the thing that has caused a decline in their sales.

Another great example of brand positioning is Silver Oak. When you think about wine, or any alcoholic beverage for that matter, your focus immediately shifts to lavish hotels or partying with friends. Silver Oak told their story as a family. They are located in California and are owned and managed by family members. Their stories connect to their audience in a very intimate manner where they show that they are a family brand, talking about the hardships they have faced while they were setting up. Even now, if you look at their Instagram page, you will find the updates are classy and showcases how their brand is focused on purity and expanding their operations.

These are examples of why it is important to determine your brand positioning before you start developing your brand story. Think of your brand as a person. Will you be sweet and polite, or snarky and sassy? Once you fix your brand personality, it will be easier for you to tell a story.

Storytelling is the best way to communicate your brand values and understand what matters to your customers. Every marketing strategy has a story at its core. This was shown very beautifully in the popular TV show *Mad Men*, where every advertising campaign was based on some story. Creative geniuses who made the catchphrases or illustrations for these advertisements always had a story behind them. They used these stories while making their pitches to their superiors, but the stories never reached the end consumer. As time has passed, consumers demand more than just the product. They want to make sure the brand they have put their faith in is worth trusting. In the 1950s or 1960s, women did not think about the ethics in the production of the lipstick they were wearing. They went to a store, looked at the best brands, picked up the shade that suited them the most, and bought it. That was it. But now, women want to know what ingredients go into the lipstick, whether harmful chemicals are used, and so on. I am not criticizing, I am simply stating that the mindset of the consumers has changed over time. Information is now more easily available, and so are choices. Consumers have become more aware, and they want to know their brands better before they swipe their cards. Just word of mouth from a salesperson is not enough for them to convince them about a brand.

With an attitude change from customers, marketing teams have to continuously come up with new ideas to keep their brands in the market. The importance of niche markets was felt more severely as people are looking for specialized products. Consumers have very specific demands, and they want their brands to come up with ideas to satisfy them, therefore marketing strategies are being altered so that brands can identify a niche market correctly. The age-old sales funnel is getting a makeover when storytelling comes into the picture. Discussions regarding core values and policies of a company, which were reserved for board meetings, are now out in the open to develop more efficient marketing strategies and create the perfect niche market.

Chapter 4:

Storytelling and Marketing Strategies

You are in your early or mid-thirties: You come from an affluent household and have been a good student with good grades and went to a good college. Now, you have a high-paying corporate job, a nice fancy car, and you have already bought your first house. You will be getting married soon and because you want to look your best for the wedding, both you and your partner decide to take up a fitness challenge. You both join a nice gym, hire a personal trainer and a nutritionist, and on your journey towards achieving fitness, you become more conscious about what you are eating. What ingredients are you using? Not only pertaining to fast-foods and your calorie intake, but also when following a strict diet.

Commercially produced vegetables are loaded with pesticides, making them unsuitable and unhealthy to eat. You have never even bothered to think about all this before now, and it was like an eye-opener for you. Both you and your partner decide to make healthier food choices, even if it means paying extra for your groceries. You don't have an affordability issue, since both of you earn good money and don't have many responsibilities now. The more you get involved in your fitness journey, the more you realize how naive you have been about the products you chose to put on your plate. You become conscious about wastage and decide to be more careful while buying essential stuff. You decide to go all organic and buy regular groceries that are procured from ethical sources.

You do your research and you come across Whole Foods, obviously not the first time you saw Whole Foods, but you began to see it in a different light after starting with your journey towards fitness and sustainable living. You read up their history, and you are impressed by how these people started their business bringing fresh, local produce to us. Not only that, they take a lot of environmentally conscious steps, such as running their stores on solar power. Even their canned tuna is sourced from traceable and sustainable stocks. So you decide to buy all your groceries from Whole Foods now. Many other brands offer organic produce, but Whole Foods is different because they are beyond a grocery brand and stand for bigger things. You are impressed by the sense of community that they try to instill within their customers, and that means a lot to you.

You are simply drawn towards all aspects of Whole Foods. The more you find out about them, you find yourself one step closer to them, making more purchases and even recommending many of their products to your relatives. Each time you go to a Whole Foods store, you pick up something new. You follow them on social media and love how they make posts about their policies and what makes them different from the rest. You are obsessed with their videos of lip-smacking delicacies made from their fresh produce.

What is a Sales Funnel?

You see what just happened here? Whole Foods drew you towards itself, without directly telling you to buy from them. It is like a funnel, where you move towards something one step at a time. Whole Foods have a very distinct customer base in their minds, and they know how to make their customers move towards them. In marketing, this is known as a "sales funnel."

A sales funnel is the breakdown of the buying process and is used by marketing experts to understand the behavior of the customers at each stage of decision-making before the purchase takes place. This helps them to understand which strategies would be effective and where they should put money. The trick to creating an effective sales funnel lies in its subtlety. It has to be a process where the customer feels they are making a conscious choice to buy this product. The marketing strategy has to work its charm without being too direct.

The funnel marketing technique is implemented in four stages:

Stage 1: Creating Awareness

Your customer needs to be aware of the product you are offering. Using computer algorithms and search engine optimization can be good to create awareness. You have to make sure the customer clicks on your ad, reads your blog, or finds out about your product from a Google search. You need to know who your customers will be, and subsequently place your advertisements in the suitable media so it gets noticed by the right customers. Many good products are lost in the sea of options, so make sure to get your product noticed.

Stage 2: Invoking Interest

You have invoked interest the customer has already clicked on the link to your product and is evaluating options. They will now compare and try to figure out whether this product is suitable for them in terms of quality and price. In this stage, it is crucial that you make the best use of storytelling and other marketing strategies because this is the phase that determines whether the customer will enter into your sales funnel or not. The more your customer is interested in your product, the better your chances of making a sale.

Stage 3: Making a Decision

Once the customer has gathered all the relevant information about your product, they will try to make a decision. It is the job of the salesperson and marketing strategies to convince the prospective buyer into buying the product. They have to use all kinds of techniques to persuade the customer. Funnel marketing promotes an indirect sales technique, but the message has to be loud and clear so that the customer can trust the product and make their decisions accordingly. Indirect does not mean ambiguous, so you have to maintain clarity in your marketing techniques.

Stage 4: The Purchase

Everything ultimately boils down to whether the customer is buying your product or not. If the buyer feels that the product is suitable for them, they will buy it. For high-priced products, they may have cold feet before making the payment. In the case of a physical sale, the salesperson can try to convince them by demonstrating further benefits of the product. In the case of websites, you will often find that they send an email if you leave a site during checkout as a way to remind and win over your customer. Even after all the efforts, you might not make the sale. No need to be disappointed, you simply have to keep following up with them and communicate yourself.

How does Storytelling Improve a Sales Funnel?

When you go for your regular haircut or the monthly grooming appointments, you usually have a specific place. Most of us even have a specific person who does our grooming, and we are usually reluctant to change that person. I don't call the salon, I call Carla, the person who cuts my hair, ask when they are available, make my appointment accordingly. It's not like they are the best personal groomer, but I trust them and I don't want anyone else to do it.

I remember when I first moved here and went into that salon, this woman came up to me and greeted me nicely. They asked me what kind of grooming I was looking for and politely made some really effective suggestions. It helped because they understood my concerns and attended to me patiently because I can be fussy. They communicated all the products available and why particular products will be suitable for me. It was not the usual demonstration by a salesperson, they told me how those products helped them and their family members. There was a sense of modesty and genuineness in their tone, which is why I liked them and continue to avail their services. Every month when I visit the salon, Carla shows me pictures of their spouse and children, and tells me stories about the antics of their pet cat. During the pandemic, when all these stores were closed, and I needed a haircut, Carla guided me through video chat and instructed me on how to trim my own hair. It was not great, but I could work with it for the time being. I have been their regular customer for almost five years now. I was drawn into the sales funnel because of their pleasant communication, honest storytelling, and eagerness to go the extra mile in times of a crisis.

Storytelling improves a sales funnel by giving it a more personal touch. In the five years that I have known Carla, I have seen them get married, have a kid, lose their mother and rescue a cat. I have developed a bond with them and that has helped them to retain me as their customer. I know there are better salons and more skilled groomers out there, but I prefer Carla because I know they provide a personal touch in their work. In order to build an efficient sales funnel, it is essential that you create this relationship with your customers, whether physically or through your online presence. Storytelling goes a long way in improving your sales funnel and here's how:

Start with the Small Talk

If you want your customer to pay attention to you and your products, you have to master the art of small talk. You will find many people complaining about how small talk is irritating. However, if you know the right topic, it is the most effective start to any conversation. Small talk is regarded as a great ritual to overcome any kind of interpersonal boundaries, which is where storytelling will help you. Stories are a great way to get the conversation rolling, be it personal or professional.

Often, the best salespersons are best because they are effortless talkers. If you are going for an online campaign, small talk can be in the form of an unrelated topic and you can gradually cue in on your main product through a series of posts. You will be able to keep your audience hooked because they do not know what's coming and this curiosity will help you to retain their attention.

Dig Up Some Dirt

If you are a good salesperson, you will know what problems your customer is facing so you can point it out to them without seeming too obvious and let them tell you more about it. At this point, you can pick up on some competitors' deficiencies and learn why you stand out. You can let your customer know that you understand their concerns and struggles are important. Take the instance of Carla, who makes it a point to let me know how they or their family members used a product before recommending it to me. Getting personal with your customers will let you get inside their inner circle of trust. They will believe you and your stories, and that will be your chance to pitch your product. They will hear you and won't find it annoying because it's not just a sales pitch, it is a recommendation by their friend.

Get Your Customer Talking

Once your customer feels comfortable with you, they will start talking with you. A dialog with your customer is a golden ticket to making sales. The beauty of storytelling is that it grows as more people share. Suppose you are selling calculators, and you tell your customer a story about that time your calculator stopped in the middle of your ninth-grade maths exam. Hearing this story, your customer also tells you about one time when one of their classmates broke their calculator during the exam and couldn't use one. You again reinstate the importance of a strong calculator and let them know how you are still not over the terror, which is why you personally make sure that your calculators are sturdy and indicate how much battery is left. Whenever your customer is talking to you, a sense of empathy is created, and you can feel the positive vibes.

Letting your customers inside a sales funnel gets easier with the help of stories. When you are using stories in your marketing strategy, you are actually opening yourself up to the vulnerabilities of your customers. Nobody likes to think they are being pushed around and forced to buy something. So, stories are the best way to persuade someone without letting them think they are being persuaded. Including a story in your marketing copy can make all the difference in your sales.

Telling a Story Through Copywriting

Copywriting is the act of writing a powerful piece of content to create awareness among potential customers and eventually lead them to purchase the product. Basically, you want to write something unique and catchy that would resonate with customers. The quality of the content is not as important as the way it is presented. A good copy can turn "I don't need this" into "I cannot do without this." To understand it more clearly, a copy is a text that you see written on billboards, newspaper headings, social media posts, and on any such media or marketing materials that a company uses to reach its customers. The importance of copywriting in any marketing campaign is unparalleled because it is what holds the campaign together. It is an important step of the sales funnel because a good copy draws us towards the brand. Nike with its iconic "Just do it" copy encourages a whole generation of people to give up being lazy and chase their dreams.

You might argue that copywriting is essentially a way to lure your customers into buying your product, so how does storytelling come into the picture? You see, when the writer is creating a copy, they want you to visualize a scene. They want to tell you a story, paint a picture in your mind so you can imagine the product as part of your life. Copywriting is a powerful tool that uses storytelling to make the message more impactful. Amidst the chaotic situation of gender bias in the workplace, the cosmetic brand L'oreal Paris came up with an advertisement targeting men, asking them to hire more women in leadership roles because they are all "worth it." L'oreal's tagline for all their products is "because we're worth it," but using the same tagline to impart a greater message is an example of a brilliant copy. Its impact was all the more aggravated because it spoke about a bigger concern and addressed the stories of thousands of women who are discriminated against in their workplace. The idea to target men was smart because L'oreal's primary audience is normally women, so when they make a copy specifically addressing men, it is bound to get noticed. Moreover, asking men to hire more women implies that it's only the men who are the bosses.

Whenever you see a good copy, there is bound to be a story behind it because without a story, it is impossible to connect with your customers. The story can be about something that causes pain to the customer, or something that brings back happy memories; your customers are always craving that special emotional connection. Have you ever wondered why Oreo cookies are one of the most popular cookies in the world? It is simply two chocolate cookies and some vanilla cream, but people go crazy over them. It is more popular than any other store-bought cookie, and every day a new recipe comes up using Oreos. Kids love it because it is fun opening up the two cookies and going for the cream first and then dunking the whole thing in milk. Adults also love it because it lets them awaken their inner child. Product quality is not the only reason why some products are more popular than others. Whenever they write an advertising copy, they make sure to include an element of relatability that transports them to a feeling of childlike innocence.

Customers feel attached to certain brands, it resonates with them because it touches their hearts. Whenever they talk about that brand, their faces light up because it is so much more than a product to them. People are sensitive, and your marketing strategy should try to focus on activating those senses within your customers. Stories are powerful because it is scientifically proven that people remember stories far more than they remember facts. It hits their brain and creates sensory activities. You must know all about that if you want your product to become popular.

What is Neuromarketing?

America has around 200 brands of bottled water. Sounds like a lot of options for something that tastes exactly the same, doesn't it? Amongst all these brands, Aquafina is the most popular. When I read these facts, I found them absurd. Water has no taste, so why do people have a favorite brand of bottled water? When you think about it carefully, you will understand that buying decisions are not always made rationally. There is only so much logic when you are picking up an Aquafina from the shelves and ignoring the other 199 brands available in front of you. Neuromarketing tries to identify the sensory neural behavior that leads a customer to make the decision to buy a particular product. Because word of mouth is not always trustworthy, neuromarketing uses scientific techniques to study brain reactions to marketing campaigns. It takes inputs from neuroscience, behavioral economics, and social psychology to develop an understanding of human reactions.

When you use neuromarketing, you can see how your customer's brain lights up (or doesn't) when they hear about your product, enabling you to understand them on a deeper level and predict their decisions. Traditional marketing experts argue that marketing campaigns succeed because they get a "gut feeling" about it, but humans don't make decisions based on their guts; it is the brain that does all the thinking and reacting, which is why it seems reasonable to study it while devising a marketing strategy. The two sides of our brain react to external stimuli in different ways. One side is cool, outgoing, and emotional, while the other is nerdy, rational, and slow. For a long time, marketing experts made an assumption that people made all their buying decisions in a rational mind, but that is not true since otherwise, people would not have been hoarding all kinds of stuff every time there is a sale. Nobody needs lipstick every two months, so rational buying behavior is mostly a myth.

Neuromarketing uses tools like functional MRIs, eye tracking, electrodermal activities, and things like that to measure whether the customer is interested in a certain product or campaign. The amount of time a customer takes to respond to questions like "Would you buy this?" is also taken into account. It helps companies to identify how they can change their product design, branding, and marketing practices as a whole to bring about an increase in sales. For example, the company Frito-Lay used neuromarketing to increase their sales amongst women. Their products had shiny outer packaging, which supposedly ignited feelings of guilt and shame in women. When you have taken a pledge of eating healthy, and you see a nice and shiny pack of crisps, you are attracted to it, but you are also feeling guilty about cheating on your diet. After Frito-Lay gathered this piece of information, they changed their packaging to a less shiny and more matte pack and saw an increase in sales.

Storytelling in Neuromarketing

Let's try to understand with an example how storytelling comes into the neuromarketing picture. Suppose you are a manufacturer and seller of smartwatches, wanting to understand how neuromarketing can help you boost your sales. You have hired an agency that specializes in this arena, and they have provided you with results about how your customers are reacting to your existing quality, packaging, and overall marketing strategy. They have also provided you with a detailed list of recommendations that could help you to improve your sales figures. There were a lot of options, but one that caught your eye was using the principle of scarcity. So you sat with your design team and came up with a new smart-watch with some features like a heart rate monitor, tension detector, and other things that would keep a track of the user's physical and mental state. While designing the advertising strategy, you decide to market these watches as "limited edition," giving the customers the feeling that they are highly specialized products manufactured in a small quantity. You follow the neuromarketing strategies and design your campaign in such a way that your customers are attracted to. You begin to post engaging social media updates regularly before the launch of the product and update your website with pictures and details of the new product, keeping focus on the fact that they are limited edition. Once the product is out in the market, results are as expected. Sales are very good because you used a scientific approach and predicted the customer's demands, but you are still confused about how following the reports of those outside people increases your sales while you and your marketing team struggle to make the same thing happen.

Now let's break it down to what actually happened. When you use neuromarketing, you are basically trying to understand what does the trick in the minds of your customers. Using a creative story to convey your marketing gimmick helps you connect with your customers. You know that. But when you insert the inputs of neuromarketing into your storytelling techniques, you are simply hitting the bullseye without making wild guesses. Going with your "gut feeling" may or may not yield the desired results. But when you have more scientific options available, showing you exactly what you can do, isn't it smarter to avail that option?

When you created your advertisement, you told your customers that your product is "limited edition," but put plenty in production and have enough inventory to last even a super-normal demand. When you project this scarcity into the minds of your customers, they feel that they need to own it; owning something that has a limited availability makes people feel special in the sense that they have something that others don't. Ultimately, everyone wants to feel a bit more special and will be willing to pay a higher price for that, which is why boutique pieces, single pieces that will not be created again, are sold at such high prices.

When you use neuromarketing, your storytelling becomes more efficient. After all, it's not a story you are sharing to impress your date, it is a story that will influence your customers to make a decision about buying your product. Your date might pretend to enjoy your stories because they like you, even if the stories are not good, your customers will not do the same which is why neuromarketing is an extremely important tool to improve your storytelling. Although it is a relatively newer branch of marketing studies, it shows great promise in predicting and targeting the specific demands of the customers.

Why Storytelling is the Best Marketing Strategy

When you want to introduce a new product in the market, you are trying to gauge the needs and demands of the customers. Until now, it had been an effort made by the company. There is a very old saying that advertising is the process that makes people buy things they do not need, which is still true. You will always find little things like gum, candy, and other small-value items kept near the checkout counters of all supermarkets. The idea behind this being that when the customer is waiting in line, they will pick up some more random stuff and the store will make a slightly bigger profit.

While these tricks are okay for small revenues, if you want to be a part of the bigger game, you need to have a skilled marketing strategy. Now more than ever, you need to be more conscious about how you are projecting yourself to your customers. A few years ago, big corporations had strict rules about dress codes, hair colors, and even visible tattoos. But now, the work culture is changing everywhere, and administrations are becoming more lenient and inclusive. The definition of being 'professional' is changing and people are looking for brands that care about them and their well-being.

Marketing is not just about creating a new demand these days, because the customers are conscious and aware. They know what they want and are looking for brands that can deliver the same to them.. Storytelling in marketing is not just about how great your company is, it is the best way to get to know your customers and your customers to know you. One of the greatest marketing strategies is the option of feedback. Many brands encourage sharing people's experiences after using a product and offer a reward for feedback, whether it is good or bad.

You are letting people know that you hear them, and taking steps to make their shopping experience better.

Stories make your marketing strategies feel more natural to your customers. Despite the very obvious product placements, when you are explaining yourself through stories, the customer is smiling instead of getting agitated. The popular music streaming app Spotify always comes up with something called "Your Summer Playlist" or "Yearly Playlist," which lists out all the songs you have played most frequently during the said span of time. Google has a similar feature where they show you snippets of whatever you searched during a year. These are great techniques for encouraging storytelling through marketing. Imagine it is the evening of 31st December. The pandemic has made it difficult to attend any parties or meet friends, so you are at home, and sitting on your couch with pizza and wine. When you see the notification from Spotify, you check it out because you are curious to know what songs you played the most. It seems like a stupid thing to do on New Years' Eve, but you have nothing better to do. When you see the playlist, you smile as you see that song you played for your virtual date. You also find a lot of songs from your common family playlist. You identify that song your mother always used to sing. You miss your parents and decide to give them a call later on. The playlist makes you happy, and after you are done scrolling through the songs, you see a flash message wishing you a happy new year, and a gentle reminder to renew your subscription. Their product placement did not annoy you although it was a direct message because Spotify made you a playlist and that playlist reminded you of all the sweet and sad times you spent during the year. There are a number of ways to include stories in your marketing campaign, whether you are a new company or an existing one. Storytelling doesn't even have to include a hero or climax, it simply has to make your customer feel warm and welcome.

Chapter 5:

Storytelling Helps A Young Business

Your new startup is ready to launch, but are your customers ready for you? How much do they know about your business? If you have a feeling that you are just starting out, and you will have plenty of time to develop your goodwill, then you are mistaken. While there are ways to develop your brand, later on, it is absolutely essential that you get off to a great start. Your success depends largely upon your customer's initial reaction to you. If you want to be a part of the market for the long haul, you have to plan before you launch yourself. Let your customers know that you are going to be a gamechanger in the industry.

Learn How to Tell Your Story

In order to build the image of a young company, storytelling is going to be an extremely important tool. By now, you already know how beneficial storytelling is and why it is essential for a successful business,but as a new startup, you might be having doubts as to how you can start using storytelling. There are various ways of telling a story, and you have to select one that you feel suits you the most. Think before you choose a storytelling technique because you will be using it for some time to come. Since you are a new business, you have to stick to a particular technique to get your customers used to your marketing strategy, helping you make a mark on the market and giving your customers the ability to identify you from the stories. A few storytelling techniques that you can use are:

Connecting the Before and After Scenarios

In this storytelling technique, you first show your customers the problem your brand is addressing, then immediately you show them their life after the solution you provide. Then, you connect the two scenarios by creating a bridge. That bridge is your product, the savior who helped the customers to solve their problems and find their happy-ever-after. The benefit of this technique is that you can show your customers you know how it feels to have the problem solved. You can give them a taste of the other side, where the grass is greener. Once you establish your knowledge about the better side, you introduce your product and show them how it can lead them to their desired destination.

Problem-Agitate-Solve

This technique also starts off by showing a problem the customers are encountering. Then you have to intensify the problem, sprinkling salt on their wounds, agitating your customers more, magnifying the problem. Remember to use emotional language and make sure the customer really feels the pain of the problem. Then present the solution and introduce your product. The objective is to portray that your product is going to bring an end to the intense suffering that your customers are going through.

Features-Advantages-Benefits

This is a textbook formula for storytelling when it comes to promoting your product. You let your customer know the features of your product, the advantages that it has, and what benefits they are going to get by using it. This method is focused on your brand and does not actively speak about the customer's demands or problems. There is very little storytelling in it because you are basically describing your product in detail to the customer. The way you say it though, is going to make all the difference. This method is very popularly used in short presentations or where there is not much scope for dramatics. It can be made really interesting with the help of correct visuals and interesting facts.

Incident-Action-Benefit

Here, you start by telling your audience a soulful story that is going to make them emotional and connect with you. You have to think of a story that would really move your customers, allowing them to relate with you. The heartfelt story will be accompanied by a problem, but you have to be discreet because you don't want your customers to think that you are making up some story to sell your product. Once the problem is established, you gently guide them towards the action they need to take to solve the problem; this is where you introduce your product without forcing it on your customers. You let them know the benefits, and let them know why your brand gives the best options.

All these technical tricks are simply for your knowledge so that you can make your storytelling more efficient. You are free to combine these techniques and make a story that sounds the best to you. The important thing is to hear your own story; if it doesn't sound convincing to you, then it won't convince your customers. Storytelling is effective in every aspect of operations and is a great tool to develop connections with your customers. A new startup will not have much reputation, so word-of-mouth publicity and high recommendations by your customers is what is going to give you a headstart.

Using Storytelling in Your Investor Pitch

Like I said, starting a business is a lot of work and the first step to get started is gathering funding. Assuming that you do not have some secret fortune hidden away, you will need to obtain funds since nothing can happen without money. Bank loans are a viable option but not if you have plans to launch a startup that is going to have huge operations; you will need funding from an external investor. Now, why should someone put their money in your business? How would you convince them that your business is worth investing towards? The best way to gain an investor's trust is by sharing your story. They would probably not want to hear about that one summer you spent with your grandparents, but they would want to know if that time somehow inspired you to come up with the idea of your startup. Tell your story properly and in a way that is relevant to your investor. Here are a few tips for using storytelling to ace an investor pitch:

Don't Bore Your Audience With Data

If you have been to an investor conference and you are pitching your idea, chances are there will be many other people doing the exact same thing to the same people. A lot of people think that talking about big numbers and weird facts will attract your investor's attention, but that is not the case. If an investor is hearing twenty pitches in a day, it is unlikely that they will remember that strange fact you might find interesting. Instead, focus on telling the story of your brand and why it is unique. Your idea is your unique selling point, not data and figures. Wrap your idea inside a good story and your investor will remember you. Apple was started in a garage by Steve Jobs and he built an empire out of that in the years to come, which is an example of the kind of data that your investor would like to hear, not how many iPhones were sold in the last year. Facts and figures are perceived by the analytical part of our brain, which eventually zones out. Stories, on the other hand, stay with us because they are absorbed by the emotional part of our brain.

Have An Element of Drama

Your story should have a certain degree of drama. Introduce your protagonist in a dramatic way and intensify their problems. Tell your investor the worst-case scenarios and make sure to overdo it just a little bit. When you are explaining your product to the investor, they are expecting a wow factor, a point where they get the benefit of your product and are genuinely impressed. In order to get to that point, you need to use your story efficiently without being carried away. It is not uncommon to become overly emotional about your product because you have put so much hard work into it. But remember that your investor doesn't want to see you breaking into tears while pitching your idea. Every aspect of storytelling should be carefully anticipated with no room for personal emotion. The objective is to ignite the emotions of the investor through dramatic elements in your storytelling.

Emphasize on Your Points

Confidence is one of the biggest factors that make your storytelling more efficient. You have to be sure about what you are saying and must be ready for any kind of uncomfortable questions. Look at it from the investor's point of view; they will be investing their money, so they have every right to ask you anything, within reason. You have to patiently answer all questions, never lose your calm, and make sure that your answers don't lack clarity. Confidently emphasize your points and avoid using hypotheticals like "can" or "could" in your pitch because it creates confusion. Suppose your startup deals with dental supplies and during your pitch, you say something like "Using this air-water syringe, you can gently clean the teeth without causing any pain." It seems like a very normal thing to say, but the investor might be someone who had a bad experience with a dentist and their mind will immediately drift to those painful nights after having a root canal. They will think "No, I would never ever use an air-water syringe!" The investor might even reject your proposal mentally for this reason. It is a good practice to use a story for emphasizing your points rather than directly addressing the investors. Your product may be something the investor does not directly relate to, and including them in the story might make them uncomfortable. You can choose to use stories from a real dentist and their patient to explain how this air water syringe is different from the others available in the market. In this way, you can let your customers know that your product is capable of being used by real people and solving real problems. The investor must have a feeling that you know what you are talking about and are up for a challenge. Your story must be able to convince your investor that your idea is worth investing in.

Be Spontaneous

The main point of telling a story is that it should not feel forced. Your investor must not think that you have memorized the story and are just letting it all out for the sake of presentation. This is why, even if you do write down your pitch, it is a good idea to not completely memorize it. You must know all the key points of your pitch and frame it accordingly. There is room for improvisation as you are telling the story, just make sure it sounds spontaneous.

Creating the perfect story for your investor pitch is not an easy task and you will not get it right the first time. Tell your story to anyone who is willing to listen and see how they react. Come up with different variations of the same story and see which one works the best. Stories have a way of getting into the hearts of people and your investors are no exceptions. Create situations within your story so that you can communicate important information to your investors without being too direct. You must avoid big figures and try to replace them with smaller and believable statistics. If you are a chatty person in general, remember this is not one of the stories you tell your friends on a Friday night over drinks. This story needs to have a purpose, a goal, and a distinct happy ending.

Marketing Tricks for Your Startup

If you are about to launch a startup now, you have to be aware of the new and modern ways to market your product. Earlier, there was a custom of sending out free samples to test a new product; still an effective way, but if you receive a bunch of free products in your mail, it is not going to impress you. You might even end up throwing them away. I remember my mother used to buy a beauty magazine every month. Sometimes they would attach samples of candies or shampoo and things like that. I used to go crazy for those things and made sure I got hold of those before anyone else. But now, kids are more likely to be excited when they receive some freebies from their favorite influencer because they won in their giveaway. Same concept, just slightly different execution. Social media has a lot of influence on customers and your marketing plan should accommodate that. Customers expect a lot from new startups in terms of demand satisfaction, sustainability, and a general code of ethics. If you have created a story for your startup, make sure your marketing strategies are in tune with that story. Your story should be consistent across all your marketing moves, helping your customers to distinguish you as a brand. Since marketing is constantly evolving, here are a few tips if you are just starting off:

Organize A Pre-Launch Giveaway

Marketing campaigns will start a few months before you actually launch your product so you can create hype about your brand. A giveaway is a great way to develop a follower base and get to know your customers. The winner of the giveaway will be rewarded with your own products, which is an excellent method to get your products sampled by customers. Giveaways are engaging campaigns since they ask each participant to follow your page, tag a few more people to the post, and in turn ask those people to follow your page. Giveaways are like the pyramid scheme of marketing strategies, except nobody is losing money and the winner is getting freebies. It is a very effective way to attract a lot of people to your brand even before the launch actually takes place.

Create Shareable Content

Instead of simple facts and figures, make your marketing messages more personalized, connecting with your customers. A customized message from the CEO or a word of advice from the financial expert makes the customers feel they are getting special treatment and are in good hands. If you start doing this from the very beginning, your brand will create a nice and friendly image for itself. Your content should be enriched with the relevant data and you will be able to target your audience more effectively. Your content must be shareable across mobile devices and tablets since people like to read things on their phones.

Write a Good Marketing Copy

Hire some good copywriters to create a powerful and impactful copy for all your advertising campaigns and social media posts. Before launching a startup, it is important that you develop the image of your brand; good copywriting can help you achieve that. If the copy in your emails, commercials, and social media posts attract your customers, it will give you a headstart in your sales.

Make Use of Visual Storytelling

My grandmother used to have a big fat recipe notebook where she would note down interesting recipes whenever she came across one. That notebook was passed down to my mother, who also added recipes to it. How many of us really look at a notebook while cooking nowadays? We simply open the video and do a virtual cook-along. Everyone has got a phone with a good camera and that is why shooting videos has never been easier. People like to watch things rather than read them because visuals give more clarity. After Instagram introduced Reels in 2020, social media went crazy and everyone started making one. Starting from dog influencers to big corporations, everyone is making reels because engagement in reels is much higher than regular picture posts.

Creating video content is the next big marketing move, and if you are a new startup you must make good use of it. With the use of relevant hashtags and geotags, you can make your video content reach a large number of people in a short time. These videos let you tell your story in a simple yet effective manner. If your launch is coming up, you can be posting stories throughout the day about how busy everything is and why you are so excited to get the product rolling. Visual storytelling is great because it is inexpensive and drives a lot of traffic to your page. You can create explainer videos to focus on the particular benefits and features of your products.

Digital marketing becomes all the more efficient when you use videos because people are impatient and will probably not read a two-page long article. If you can get them hooked though, they might watch a ten-minute-long video. Have you ever come across those painting videos or videos where a crew is cleaning some really dirty places? There is something oddly satisfying about watching an old and worn-out teddy bear getting squeaky clean and you could watch that stuff for hours. Videos are a great way to publicize your brand because if you can make it interesting, people will watch it.

Hosting or Joining A Podcast

Podcasts are the new marketing obsession. You can choose to start a new podcast or appear in an existing one. Podcasts usually take place weekly, so every week you get to share your insights about the market with your potential customers. If you are camera conscious or feel that you are not good with shooting videos, podcasts might just be your thing. It will help you reach a big customer base and reinstate what you have already explained in your blog. Podcasts are a nice way to tell your story to the customers because it is like directly speaking to the audience.

Create a Rewarding Recommendation System

Word of mouth publicity is still one of the best ways to get yourself noticed, but why would people publicize your product? You have to give your customers some incentive if you want them to recommend your products to others. While some people might automatically ask their friends or family to use your product, it is better if you don't leave that to chance and set up a solid rewarding recommendation system. It could be something like giving each person a unique code and link, and if anybody joins your community or buys a product, both these people will get freebies or discounts on their purchases, helping you connect to more people and create better relationships with your customers.

Set up an Email Marketing Campaign

No matter how much social media gets popularized, there is nothing more effective than an email marketing campaign. All professionals check their emails multiple times a day and sending newsletters and updates via email will easily capture their attention. You can choose to set up an automated email system that will simply send emails to all subscribers at regular frequencies. Automated emails are very efficient because you do not have to draft emails every time, you can simply set up a system with a network and the work will be done. You can send numerous updates and newsletters with the help of an automated email system that will reach your customers. Quality emails are bound to get the right attention and increase conversion rates.

A lot of people often wonder what the point is of introducing a new product or startup. There are already so many products in the market, how will this one be anything different? The market is now saturated with thousands of products in the same category with little or no variation, but does that mean you should stop making new things? Definitely not. There may be millions of products on the market, but there are also millions of new ways to make your product unique. Branding and packaging are reaching new heights every day and there is always something different happening with social media promotions. Coca-Cola is promoting recycling of its existing bottles so that they can come up with Smartwater, which would come in bottles made of 100% recycled plastic. Skincare brands are coming up with vintage packaging of their products so that the customers get the benefit of the new wrapped in some old-school charm.

Cupcakes and truffles have been around for ages. Bakeries run smoothly because everyone loves a good cheesecake or some freshly baked bread. But with rising consciousness about obesity, people started taking rain checks on desserts because buying a whole cake would mean too much of a calorie intake. A slice of pastry is always available, but it doesn't stay fresh for very long, thus, bakers came up with the idea of dessert jars. For people who want to watch their weight, it is a great option because it is of lesser quantity and comes in a covered glass jar where the freshness remains intact.

The health-conscious consumers were still not satisfied, because even if the quantity is less, it is still sugar and carbs. So bakers and nutritionists came up with healthier options for the dessert jars like chia pudding, oatmeal crumbles, and frozen yogurt smoothies. As more and more people came up with their ideas and variations of these desserts, newer and improved products started entering the market and guess what, all of them are successful because they were curated after listening to the concerns and stories of the people. Maybe somebody makes a thicker smoothie and likes to have it in a bowl instead of a glass and pretend they are having a dessert. Some healthy baker sees this and comes up with the idea of smoothie jars and tells the customers that it is exactly like a dessert, minus the calories.

The digital world is taking us to new heights every day and making unexpected changes in the market. A lot of companies now use augmented reality to market their products. A few years ago, when online shopping was just starting, people were skeptical about buying certain products online. For example, they felt that when buying lipstick or nail polish, they would want to physically check the shade and see how it looks on them and would ask for a sample color to be tested and swatched on them. But now, even while shopping online, you can virtually try shades before buying them. You can upload a picture of your face and the website will show you how that particular shade will look on you. This technology is used by a lot of high-end salons as well, where if you select a haircut, or a style or beard, they will use a picture of your face and show you how it will look on you. That way there will be no surprises for you, and the chance of looking stupid with a new hairdo is reduced.

New products and niche markets are being identified every day with the development of new technology and strategies. Social media has also helped companies understand the stories and choices of their customers. If you notice carefully what people are posting on social media, you will find a lot of insights about their problems and what they are looking for. That is your market research right there. The center of all marketing is on the internet because people are always glued to their phones. This is why it is of utmost importance that you develop a proper website for your startup or blog. A well-developed website is a key to all your marketing strategies to succeeding, and for people to know your story.

Chapter 6:

A Good Website Tells A Good Story

You have bought a new phone, and now you want to click pictures of everything. You particularly enjoy clicking pictures of food, but your crockeries are not nearly good enough to pursue what you see in the pictures so you decide to buy some nice ceramic plates and bowls. You don't want the regular ones that are available at big retailers, you are trying to be sustainable and want to shop from someone local. Your friend had told you that a lot of small local shop owners have pages on Instagram where they display their products, so you search for them and find some pretty impressive results. There was one particular page that you really liked, and it had the kind of things you were looking for. The prices were not mentioned in the posts. There was a nice caption along with the information that if anyone wanted to purchase these items, they had to send a direct message to this page or click on the link given in their bio. You sent them a text, but there was no response for a couple of days. You really liked the products so you decided to check out their website. Once you clicked on the link, you were directed to a really ill-designed website. The products were not displayed in proper order, there was no filter available, and you couldn't even see the prices. What made matters worse was that the site kept crashing and it redirected you to the main page. You got pretty annoyed and decided you are not going to buy from here after all. Your experience with the website made you think they were most likely not professional people. Their products are good, but what if there is some problem after you purchase them? They are already not replying, and their website looks terrible. How can you expect that they will provide any good service? You closed the website and unfollowed the page, the bad website turning you away from the good products.

Why a Website is Essential for Business Growth

Recent years have shown that E-commerce is the biggest thing to happen to us and it is here to stay. With the pandemic hitting us, and restrictions being imposed on free movement, the entire marketplace has moved online. From socks to sausages, lipstick to locks, everything is available online. In the days to come, the online marketplace will grow even more because of its convenience and ease of use. With one-click returns and easy exchanges, online shopping has become the best option for most people. Not only products, but all major service providers also have their websites from which people can book their services. Newspapers and books have come to our phones and computers, which which is why, no matter what you are creating, a good website is absolutely essential to ensure the success of your brand.

All the while, we have been talking about how storytelling is important for the growth of a business. When you have a good story, a website will help you to showcase that story better to your customers. A good website adds value and credibility to your stories and makes your business shine brighter. When you tell your customers a good story about your brand, your customers start expecting very big things from you. A lot of brands think that an active social media presence is enough, but that's not the case. In order to be taken seriously, you have to build a well-developed and informative website and its benefits are many.

Constant Online Presence and Support

The best thing about having a website is that you get to have a constant online presence. Your website is always accessible to anybody anywhere in the world. Websites also enable you to provide customer service always. Your website must have a section for frequently asked questions to solve most of the customer queries. Apart from that, many websites are now equipped with chatbots, which are virtual assistants that help customers with more specific queries. You can use chatbots to provide additional information on registration and new products. Even after business hours, your customers will be able to get their queries solved through the websites.

Availability of Information

If you call somebody about a new product your company is launching, chances are that the person will tell you to send them an email or provide the link to your website so they can check it out themselves. People today do not have the patience to listen to a new product over the phone. They would rather click on the link and find out what offers your company is providing and which ones are beneficial for them. All information regarding your company and products or services must be available on your website for easy access.

Reduce Costs

A lot of companies nowadays prefer to have online stores only because a physical store is more expensive and involves a lot of hassles. If you have adequate space for storing your inventory, there is not much need for a physical store. Creating a website through content management services like WordPress is very simple and cost-effective. Websites are also essential for service providers and content creators because that is the best platform to increase your reach without burning a hole in your finances. A physical store will have visibility within a specific radius, but your website will be available to anyone in the world at a much lesser price.

Storytelling Redefined

Websites are a great platform to take your brand storytelling to the next level. You can include testimonials from happy customers who have been satisfied with your product or service. You can add comments from your employees who will express how happy they are to be working with you and how high work ethics are followed. Your brand story will be redefined through your website and you will be able to communicate your values even better. Suppose you are a travel company that specializes in heritage tourism: You can make a video of all the historical places you visited with your team in the last 6 months, including beautiful visuals of each destination and recorded experiences of the people who went on these trips with your company. You can enrich your brand story with these insights and your potential customers can get an idea about the kind of company they will be dealing with.

If you are a company that has developed a great brand story and an active social media presence, a well-developed website is essential for you. When you tell your customers a good story about yourself, they expect bigger things from you. Suppose your social media account is filled with posts about how much your company values your customer's time and why their service is always perfect. You have a very righteous image on the internet and when a customer clicks on your website, they are unable to find the right thing and they end up wasting a lot of their time in vain. Simply telling your story and publicizing it is not enough, you must have the right means to back it up.

Developing a Good Website

The first step to be covered while you are developing a website for your company is to create the content for it. The content must be customer-oriented and should avoid redundant information. Content is the most important thing, whether you are selling something or you have a blog that people use for educational purposes; make sure your content is easy to understand and relevant for your customers. The content is the base of your website and your layout and the rest of the technicalities will depend on it. Here are a few helpful tips for developing a good website.

Tips on Content

There has been a constant focus on how to tell your story in a profitable manner. Now is the time to implement it through your website content. Communicate your story and values to your customers in a precise but effective manner, your website content should reflect on what you stand for as a brand. Do not provide any false information or exaggeration. Forget about your high school English essay, your website does not need flowery language or difficult phrases. Use conversational English that people will relate to and understand. Everything that your customer needs must be properly visible on the website. Your content must contain a call-to-action, and for that to happen, make sure to include all contact information for you and your company. Develop content that would help your customers trust you and create a good image of your company. You can add visuals like videos and pictures to make the content more appealing. Another effective tip to make your website more efficient is to keep updating the information. You will often see many websites have two dates, one when it was originally published and one when it was last updated. If a reader or customer finds that your content was recently updated, that means your website has the latest information on the particular topic, making your website content more trustworthy.

Technical Development Tips

Once you have developed your content, it is time to select a platform for your website. Those days of developing a website using difficult HTML codes are gone because website development has become very easy now. Content Management Systems like WordPress have made it very easy for normal people to create and manage their own content on their websites. Development tips are incomplete without sharing the benefits of WordPress with you: The best thing about WordPress is that it is free. Unlike other web development platforms, it does not charge you anything to create or develop content. You can customize it according to your needs and it is highly efficient. It helps to make your website responsive, which means your page will look just as good on mobiles. Because WordPress is used by a large number of bloggers and small-business owners all over the world, there is a very helpful community always available in case you have any difficulty.

After you have selected a platform, you will need a domain name and a host for your website. A domain name is your website name, the one that will appear in the address bar in your browser. Choosing a short and catchy domain name is great for people to remember. Your domain name should match your company name so that it is more visible and easy to find. A host is a service that will connect your site to the internet. Choosing an efficient host service is essential to avoid website crashes or frequent reloading. Both domain name and host services will cost you around $3.00 to $5.00 a month. Although free domain names are available, it is advisable to choose a paid one to look more professional.

Tips on Layout

Make your website easy to understand. The contact information should be clearly visible on top and in other distinct areas. Your website layout should be simple and not cluttered, do not include too much useless information and use short paragraphs and bullet points for better clarity. The design should not be anything too complicated or flooded with too many pictures, too many visuals may divert your customer's attention from the important information. Navigation should be proper in your website, meaning movement between various tabs of the website should not be clumsy. A lot of websites have tabs like "move to the top" visible at the side when the reader has scrolled down to the end of the page.

Tips on Generating Leads

A website is your gateway to increasing sales, and you should focus on that particularly. Do not think that just because you have developed a website, your sales will increase automatically. Dedicate a specific time every day for generating new leads for web design and acquiring new clients. Your website must contain figures and testimonials indicating that your business is successful, helping to attract new web design leads. Make sure you can also know who is inquiring about your business. There is no point in spending a lot of money designing the website and developing its content if the people are not feeling comfortable inquiring about your product or service. Suppose you have a section where the customer can provide their information and request a callback. A customer is visiting your website, and when they come to this point, they either back off because they are feeling hesitant or they simply don't feel like feeding all that information in there. In order to avoid this and make your website more useful to your customers, you can have a kind of quote calculator that would help them to find out how much your service would cost them. This way, they do not have to talk to you right away and can figure out for themselves whether your product or service is affordable for them. Make your website interactive with a number of lead capture forms so that you can turn your users into leads.

Tips on Increasing Visibility

You can have a well-designed website with top-notch content, but that would become useless unless people can find it. Incorporate SEO best practices, which stands for "search engine optimization," meaning that your website will be visible on the first page of Google or any search engine when people search for anything relating to your product. All search engines have algorithms, or keywords, that increase the visibility of a particular website. The first step in determining your position on a search engine is crawling. If the link to your website appears on many other sites, chances are high that people will find your site through clicking on them. After the initial crawling, search engines index your website and analyze them for fresh and relevant content including layouts and visuals. The better your content, the better your chances of getting a higher ranking. When you search for something, the first result you find always has the most relevant and fresh content because it went through the steps to search engine optimization. Be it school or website, it always helps to have a top rank.

If you are a content creator, it may be difficult for you to start earning from your website. It takes time for people to notice your blog. In the initial days, engagement will be low and money will not be sufficient, so you have to find other ways to earn money through your blog. This is where affiliate marketing comes into the picture. If you are selling something, you can use affiliate marketing as a means of indirect business promotion at a much lower cost than usual marketing channels.

Making Money from Affiliate Marketing

Suppose you sell kitchen equipment, and you have a couple of stores but business has not been very good ever since the pandemic hit because people are not visiting the stores anymore. You have a website and you provide online shopping, but you feel your products are not reaching your customers. Your store was always full of customers, so you know that people like your products. Now, you are learning more about digital marketing because the entire marketplace has shifted to the internet and in order to survive, you have to upgrade yourself. Apart from developing your website and promoting your page on social media, you decide to get in touch with chefs, food bloggers, and bakers who have blogs and share recipes online. You provide them with a few pieces of your equipment and ask them to use them in their videos. When they shoot the videos, they will mention that the wok or spatula is from your store and provide links to your website on their blog and below their videos. This way, if someone likes the product, they can click on it and land on your website; affiliate marketing in a nutshell.

Affiliate marketing helps business owners to grow and reach a greater audience. The business owner can associate themselves with affiliates (the bloggers in the above cases), who will promote their products on their pages. If a customer clicks on the link of the affiliate and makes a purchase, the affiliate is rewarded with a commission. The business makes a sale, the customer gets their desired product, and everyone is happy. Even if the customer does not make a purchase immediately, they are entering into the sales funnel and would have your product in mind for later.

Benefits of Affiliate Marketing to Business Owners

If you are just starting your business, there are chances you will not be equipped with a proper sales and marketing team. If you are availing of affiliate marketing techniques, you will simply have to take the initial effort to select a suitable affiliate. The rest of the marketing is done by the affiliate and you will enjoy the benefits the same. Having an affiliate marketing team will reduce your costs of marketing. The charges for domain and website hosting will be borne by your affiliate and you have to pay them only when they make a sale as opposed to a fixed salary. The lower cost you are incurring, the lower your risk. Affiliate marketing involves almost no risk on the part of the business owner and is ideal for someone who has just started and cannot afford to incur big expenses. Business owners get access to their targeted customers which in turn helps them find their niche market. Affiliate marketing offers flexibility and high returns because there is a minimum investment involved. It also helps them with search engine optimization and increases the visibility of their brand.

Benefits of Affiliate Marketing to Bloggers

Affiliate marketing is a convenient income source for most content creators because they do not have to do much for it. There is no investment involved on their part and the risk is also low. However, if they manage to make good sales through their website, they will be able to develop a good relationship with the advertisers and get the opportunity to become affiliates for more products. Since it is an online platform, they will not need to store any products with them, once the customer is interested in making a purchase, they will be directed to the advertiser's website. The affiliate earns a commission for every sale, and if they are good marketers, these commissions can very well become the main source of their income.

Benefits of Affiliate Marketing to Customers

Influencers have more followers on social media than any brand and they are always recommending good products on their feed. Most influencers act as affiliates for their niche and the customers get the benefit of good recommendations through them. Customers are always attracted by the fancy stuff that the influencers are using and want to buy what they have. Affiliates put detailed reviews and information about the products they are advertising, making it easier for the customer to choose their favorites. They also provide information about the best prices and upcoming sale offers. Customers get the benefit of information from affiliate marketing.

Let us take the instance of a lifestyle blogger: This is a woman in her late thirties. She is married and has two kids, a working mom, with a full-time corporate job. She posts updates about the various things happening in her life, starting from buying a new house to having a second child. There are detailed videos, posts, and blogs about her life and the struggles she faces. Although it sounds pretty boring and mundane, she has over two hundred thousand followers because she presents herself in a very likable manner. She is the typical American woman who everyone relates to. She regularly makes recommendations of all the things she buys or thinks would benefit her customers. If she's wearing a new shade of lipstick, she will attach the link for it. If she bought a new kitchen cabinet, she will attach the link for it. This is a woman who is telling her story every day through her blog and social media posts. The other day she posted about how she started off with a juice cleanse only to give up on it the second day. It was making her too hungry, so she whipped up some pancakes for herself. She attached links to the cleanse that she failed to follow, and all the ingredients and equipment she used to make the pancakes. She has a very likable social media image because she is not perfect, she is just like the rest of us. Subsequently, the brands she chooses to attach herself to get the benefit of being her favorite. People are thinking that if she is recommending it, the product must be good.

Stories have this immense impact on people and it makes them think from their heart. There is no reason for you to rely upon the recommendations of a person you don't know, but you do it anyway because she chose to make you a part of their story. The brands she is an affiliate with also make an impression on the customers without actually doing anything. The only thing the brand needs to do is develop itself in such a way that it does not disappoint the customer. The customer is already impressed with you because of the affiliate, you simply have to develop a good website to keep them captivated. You have to make sure you both are a part of your story. Wherever the customer is, they must feel that your product is worth investing in and your website is the way to make sure of that.

Your website is how the world sees you. Your company may be based in America, but someone from Sri Lanka can be interested in the product you are selling. The website is the only connection that the two of you have, and that is why it is important to create one that will be easily accessible to anyone in the world. Your information should be relevant and people must not feel that there are any territorial restrictions. The main point of globalization is to overcome the territorial barriers and free flow of goods and services. Your company's website will help people all over the world to know you, and it will allow you to know their concerns. It lets you understand them, and lets them feel that their stories are being heard. When they click on your link, you let them inside your world and they let you inside theirs. A connection is made that is deeper than just a financial transaction. That is why it's called a link, isn't it?

Conclusion

I once watched an episode of a popular TV show where two salesmen had gone to make a sales pitch to a potential client. The two of them were different kinds of people. One was sweet, amiable, the kind of guy you would like immediately. The other guy was the weird one, there can not be any other description for him. When these two guys reached the client's office, the sweet one started speaking to the client and informed him about their prices and what discounts they can offer, usual sales pitch stuff. The other weird guy asked the client whether he could use his phone. The client agreed, although it was a strange request by a salesman. But then again, the guy was weird so he let it be. The client was mostly talking to the other guy because that is where the real conversation was going on. The scene was set like this: The client speaking to one salesman and the other salesman is busy on the phone. Just when the discussion came to prices, the client told them that he was satisfied with everything but. Since they were a mid-sized company, their prices were not as good as a big corporation. The sweet salesman was explaining how they could work out a discount and how they would always be available in case of any need. Just when he opened the topic of customer service, the other guy looks at his watch and lets the customer know that he is on the phone for almost half an hour with no response. The client is confused and asks him what he's talking about and the weird salesman said he had made a call to the customer service department of the big corporation he was talking about, the one who gave better prices. It has been half an hour, and his call is still in the queue. Nobody has picked up the call and it is likely that nobody will. Then he hangs up the phone and makes a call to their company's customer service. The call is picked up immediately by their representative, asking the caller how they may be of assistance. He keeps the phone and the other sweet guy tells the client that this is what they mean when they say they will always be there for their clients. The big corporation might offer slightly lower prices, but the client will not get any help in case of an emergency. They will only tell the client to wait and that their "call is very important" to them. The client was obviously impressed and they aced the sale. So you see how they set up the scene and smoothly got their point across. It was true that they could not compete with the prices of a big company, but they make up for it with their personal assistance and customer support. With their teamwork and pitch, everything was perfect. Had they not used this setup, the client would never have been convinced.

What I am trying to explain through this story is that you can use storytelling in any aspect of your business. There is no need to think that you have to come up with a grand story for your brand marketing campaign, it is equally effective everywhere, but you already know that because you made it this far. The beauty of a story is that you don't even have to ask your customers to buy your product, they will do it automatically once they connect with you. The arena of marketing is very wide and there are a million strategies you can use for your startup. The greatest marketing strategy though, is telling a story that will resonate with your customers. You have been telling and listening to stories since childhood, but telling the story of your brand is different. That is why it is necessary to understand the intricacies and technicalities of brand storytelling.

Customers have become aware and they look at the back of the package before buying a product. Did you know that products that don't have the complete ingredient list at the back of their labels get bad reviews? People think that if the ingredients are not mentioned then they must have added too many preservatives or harmful chemicals they don't want to disclose. A few decades ago, brands would not have even given a thought about that. Now the world is changing and you have to up your marketing game if you want to keep up with the competition. Marketing and advertising were mostly dominated by visionary men who had great instincts about what the people are going to like. You cannot take the risk of depending only on instincts because people have dynamic demands. Everything you do and say is going to be pinned to your image, so it is important to be inclusive. Every year the month of June is celebrated as Pride Month' all over the world. All popular brands put up the rainbow flag next to their logo in celebration of Pride. It might sound like an inclusive move, but if you read articles by the LGBTQIA+ community, you will find they do not see this as welcoming. Confused? Let's understand it from a deeper perspective. If your company is simply putting up a rainbow flag during June, it is a show-off. You do not care about the real cause and you are doing it as a marketing gimmick. Your customers will sense the lack of genuineness and brand you as a fake. If you really want to project your brand as inclusive, you have to share personal stories of how your company does not discriminate against people based on their race, gender, or sexuality. Don't be afraid to be personal with your customers. Express your concerns and be vulnerable with them. Don't fall for the popular stances, develop your own voice with the help of your original story.

David Bowie saw a couple near the Berlin Wall with such love in their eyes and got the inspiration to write his song *Heroes*. Four decades later, the song still remains a favorite, not just for the music and lyrics but the story hidden within them. Distressed lovers still connect with the song and consider themselves to be a part of it. That is why stories are always remembered, whether it is a song or a product. People want to know how you came up with the product and the story behind it. The marketing game has changed drastically over the last few years, and the only way you can make yourself stand out is by telling your story. A marketing strategy can be imitated, but not your story. If you pour your heart out to your customers, they are bound to be overwhelmed. The results will be splendid, both financially and socially. After all, telling a story is not about making sales, it's about winning hearts.

I hope my insights about storytelling were useful to you. If you liked what you read, please leave a review on Amazon.

References

6 Benefits of Affiliate Marketing. (2020, December 15). Impact Networking. https://www.impactmybiz.com/blog/benefits-of-affililate-marketing/

Author, G. (2018, October 11). Brand Storytelling, Defined. Marketing Insider Group. https://marketinginsidergroup.com/strategy/brand-storytelling-defined/

Baran, A. (2018, July 27). How the Art of Storytelling Can Help Marketers With Brand Positioning. SEOptimer: SEO Audit & Reporting Tool. White Label Option. https://www.seoptimer.com/blog/the-art-of-storytelling-and-brand-positioning/

Bernazzani, S. (2017, November 27). 12 of the Sassiest Brands on Social Media. Blog.hubspot.com. https://blog.hubspot.com/marketing/sassiest-social-media-brands

Bisson, B. (2020, September 28). How to Benefit from Affiliate Marketing. Business Town. https://businesstown.com/benefit-affiliate-marketing/

Blog, R. (2020, June 7). Tips for Building A Brand Story That Resonates With Your Customers. Medium. https://medium.com/@neha.naik_13364/tips-for-building-a-brand-story-that-resonates-with-your-customers-9dd761cd4368

C&EN Media Group. (2018, September 20). The Last Step of Your Neuromarketing Guide: Storytelling that Moves Your Audience to Action. C&EN Media Group. https://acsmediakit.org/blog/the-last-step-of-your-neuromarketing-guide-storytelling-that-moves-your-audience-to-action/

Carter, E. (n.d.). 9 Niche Marketing Examples. https://www.webfx.com/

Chan, J. (2018, September 10). 3 Reasons Visual Storytelling is Perfect for Small Business Marketing. Keap.com. https://keap.com/business-success-blog/marketing/content-marketing/visual-storytelling

Costa, C. D. (n.d.). Why Every Business Needs Powerful Storytelling To Grow. Forbes. Retrieved August 14, 2021, from https://www.forbes.com/sites/celinnedacosta/2017/12/19/why-every-business-needs-powerful-storytelling-to-grow/?sh=a45c7ff43b0b

Costa, C. D. (2019, January 31). 3 Reasons Why Brand Storytelling Is The Future Of Marketing. Forbes. https://www.forbes.com/sites/celinnedacosta/2019/01/31/3-reasons-why-brand-storytelling-is-the-future-of-marketing/?sh=5fb29ae655ff

DeMain, B. (2019, February 4). The Story Behind The Song: Heroes by David Bowie. Classic Rock Magazine; Louder. https://www.loudersound.com/features/the-story-behind-the-song-heroes-by-david-bowie

Dennis. (2020, December 8). StackPath. Www.coredna.com. https://www.coredna.com/blogs/b2b-storytelling

Deroy, J. (2018, September 27). Storytelling in the sales funnel. Www.linkedin.com. https://www.linkedin.com/pulse/storytelling-sales-funnel-jerome-deroy

Dublino, J. (2021, July 23). 10 Tips for Building an Effective Business Website. Www.businessnewsdaily.com. https://www.businessnewsdaily.com/9811-effective-business-website-tips.html

Durdag, Y. (2020, August 12). Brand storytelling: How to sell more with the proven 7-step framework. GrowForce. https://www.grow-force.com/brand-storytelling-framework/

Eisenberg, S. (2019, November 12). 10 Examples of Highly Effective Niche Marketing Strategies. Www.wrike.com. https://www.wrike.com/blog/niche-marketing-strategies/

Evans, M. (n.d.). Storytelling in Marketing: A Way To Be Remembered. Wynter.com. Retrieved August 14, 2021, from https://wynter.com/post/storytelling

Gioglio, J., & Walter, E. (n.d.). 3 Brilliant Examples of Brand Storytelling You May Have Missed. https://www.convinceandconvert.com/

Goodwin, C. (2020, August 1). Storytelling To Reach Your Niche. Cathygoodwin.com. https://cathygoodwin.com/storyniche/

Green, S. (2019, January 9). 15 Tips to Create Killer Website Content - Susan Greene Copywriter. Susan Greene Copywriter. https://www.susangreenecopywriter.com/articles/15-tips-killer-content.html

Griffin, B. (2019, June 18). What is Copywriting? | DigitalMarketer. DigitalMarketer. https://www.digitalmarketer.com/blog/what-is-copywriting/

Hayes, M. (2019, May 1). Affiliate Marketing: How to Turn Product Recommendations Into Passive Income. Shopify. https://www.shopify.in/blog/affiliate-marketing

How Whole Foods Started an Organic Revolution and Became a $13 Billion Company. (2018, August 6). Product Habits.

https://producthabits.com/how-whole-foods-started-an-organic-revolution-and-became-a-13-billion-company/

Hultman, J., Hermansson, E., & Na, J. (2008). How Does a Company Communicate Through Storytelling? . https://www.diva-portal.org/smash/get/diva2:132493/fulltext01

Katai, R. (2019, July 24). Corporate Storytelling: What it is and Why it's Important. ROBERT KATAI. https://robertkatai.com/corporate-storytelling/

Keane, L. (2018, April 23). 10 Examples of Brand Storytelling (with Data) that Hit the Mark. GWI. https://blog.gwi.com/marketing/brand-storytelling/

Klotz, K. (2016, February 16). 7 Ways to Make Your Business Storytelling Awesome. Content Marketing Consulting and Social Media Strategy. https://www.convinceandconvert.com/digital-marketing/make-business-storytelling-awesome/

Kosaka, K. (2018, January 18). Here's How to Handle Niche Marketing. Plus, 3 Examples to Get You Started. Alexa Blog; Alexa Blog. https://blog.alexa.com/niche-marketing/

Kristina. (2021, March 31). 9 Best Value Proposition Examples + How to Create One. https://sixads.net/blog/value-proposition-examples/

Landes, E. (2020, September 9). Copywriting vs. Storytelling: How to Use One to Benefit the Other. Medium. https://writingcooperative.com/copywriting-vs-storytelling-how-to-use-one-to-benefit-the-other-a5f8973d9511

Lier, C. (2020, February 26). Get Quality Web Design Leads in 4 Simple Steps without spending on Ads. LeadGen App. https://leadgenapp.io/what-is-the-best-way-to-generate-leads-for-website-design/

Maday, J. (2020, January 8). What is Neuromarketing? How Your Brain Responds to Branding. The Future of Customer Engagement and Experience. https://www.the-future-of-commerce.com/2020/01/08/neuromarketing-definition/

Mening, R. (2018, November 24). How to Make a Website. How to Make a Website. https://websitesetup.org/

Neef, R. (n.d.). Stories Sell: 5 Proven Storytelling Techniques For Marketing Copywriters. Www.zerys.com. Retrieved August 30, 2021, from https://www.zerys.com/writers/writers-blog/bid/94332/stories-sell-5-proven-storytelling-techniques-for-marketing-copywriters

Niki, A. (2016a, July 21). How to Nail the Pitch: 17 Storytelling Tips for Startups. The Founder Institute. https://fi.co/insight/how-to-nail-the-pitch-17-storytelling-tips-for-startups

Niki, A. (2016b, July 21). How to Nail the Pitch: 17 Storytelling Tips for Startups. The Founder Institute. https://fi.co/insight/how-to-nail-the-pitch-17-storytelling-tips-for-startups

Panel, E. (2021, February 10). Council Post: Eight Steps To Take To Determine Your Niche And What Makes Your Brand Stand Out. Forbes. https://www.forbes.com/sites/theyec/2021/02/10/eight-steps-to-take-to-determine-your-niche-and-what-makes-your-brand-stand-out/?sh=39462f3547de

Pearce, J. (2017, April 30). How to Use Storytelling to Build a Sales Funnel. GrowMap. https://growmap.com/storytelling-build-a-sales-funnel/#how_to_find_your_story

Pre-Launch Your Business with Gleam. (n.d.). Gleam.io. Retrieved August 19, 2021, from https://gleam.io/guides/prelaunch

Rampton, J. (2017, November 7). A 5-Step Formula To Find Your Niche. https://www.forbes.com/

Rothman, D. (n.d.). The Art of Social Sharing: 5 Social Campaign Ideas to Get Your Audience Engaged. https://blog.marketo.com/

SBI. (2017, September 25). Why Good Storytelling Beats Good Selling. Salesbenchmarkindex.com. https://salesbenchmarkindex.com/insights/why-good-storytelling-beats-good-selling/

Six Inspiring Examples Of Neuromarketing Done Right. (n.d.). Honchosearch. https://www.honchosearch.com/blog/digital-content/why-storytelling-important-marketing-2020/

Smith, L. (2021a, April 4). 8 Ways to Tell Your Most Compelling Brand Story. Www.wordstream.com. https://www.wordstream.com/blog/ws/2018/11/08/brand-story

Smith, L. (2021b, May 2). The 16 Best Marketing Strategies to Try in 2020. Www.wordstream.com. https://www.wordstream.com/blog/ws/2020/01/07/best-marketing-strategies

Smith, L. (2021c, July 8). 21 Off-the-Charts Impressive Copywriting Examples. Wordstream.com. https://www.wordstream.com/blog/ws/2019/09/03/copywriting-examples

Staff, W. M. (2021, May 14). Different Ways Storytelling Can Inform Your Marketing Strategy. The Wise Marketer - Featured News on Customer Loyalty and Reward Programs. https://thewisemarketer.com/loyalty-strategy/storytelling-marketing-strategy/

The. (2019). Definition of Niche Marketing | What is Niche Marketing ? Niche Marketing Meaning - The Economic Times. The Economic Times. https://economictimes.indiatimes.com/definition/niche-marketing

The Importance of Storytelling in Growing Your Business - TechnologyAdvice. (2018, March 22). TechnologyAdvice. https://technologyadvice.com/blog/sales/the-importance-of-storytelling-in-growing-your-business/

The Last Step of Your Neuromarketing Guide: Storytelling that Moves Your Audience to Action. (2018, September 20). C&EN Media Group. https://acsmediakit.org/blog/the-last-step-of-your-neuromarketing-guide-storytelling-that-moves-your-audience-to-action/

Thompson, S. (2018, December 7). The importance of storytelling in business, with examples. Virtualspeech.com; VirtualSpeech. https://virtualspeech.com/blog/importance-storytelling-business

Waites, C. (2020, January 6). Why Storytelling in Marketing is Important in 2020. Honchō. https://www.honchosearch.com/blog/digital-content/why-storytelling-important-marketing-2020/

Ward, S. (2018). The Trick to Capitalizing on a Niche Market & 3 of the Most Popular. The Balance Small Business. https://www.thebalancesmb.com/niche-market-definition-for-business-2947188

What is a Niche Market? 7 Niche Market Examples. (n.d.). https://www.ownr.co/

What is a Sales Funnel? | Keap. (n.d.). Keap.com. https://keap.com/product/sales-funnel

What Is Affiliate Marketing And Its Benefits. (n.d.). Engaio Digital. https://engaiodigital.com/affiliate-marketing/

What Is Brand Storytelling and Why Does it Matter? (n.d.). Kapost. https://uplandsoftware.com/kapost/resources/blog/why-does-brand-storytelling-matter/

Zottola, J. (2020, April 2). Why Storytelling Is Such A Powerful Communications Strategy. Stern Strategy Insights. https://insights.sternstrategy.com/brand-storytelling-powerful-marketing/

www.ingramcontent.com/pod-product-compliance
Lightning Source LLC
Chambersburg PA
CBHW052332220526
45472CB00001B/392